THE

UNITED STATES

ILLUSTRATED;

IN

VIEWS

OF

CITY AND COUNTRY.

WITH

DESCRIPTIVE AND HISTORICAL ARTICLES,

EDITED

BY

CHARLES A. DANA.

NEW YORK:—HERRMANN J. MEYER.

THE WEST;

OR,

THE STATES OF THE MISSISSIPPI VALLEY,

AND

THE PACIFIC.

ADVERTISEMENT.

WHILE the scenery of the older parts of the Union has already afforded subjects for Illustrated works of greater or less excellence, the magnificent and characteristic field of the Great West has remained comparatively unexplored. The Artists whose sketches our engravers now present to the public, accordingly enjoy the advantage of depicting nature in her utmost freshness, as well as grandeur.

It would be difficult to find Landscapes of more novel and imposing features than are presented along the River Mississippi, especially in the upper portion of its course; or in the mighty reach of territory which extends thence to the Pacific, including California and Oregon. Even those who suppose themselves familiar with every portion of the Union, will find in the Illustrations we offer for their inspection that some of the most magnificent and peculiar regions of the world have been unknown to them. With regard to every important point in this vast extent of country, we are confident that they will also find authentic and valuable information in the pages that follow, whose authors write not from the report of others, but from their own observations and experience.

THE

UNITED STATES ILLUSTRATED

EDITED BY

CHARLES A. DANA.

PUBLISHED BY

HERRMANN J. MEYER, NEW-YORK.

TABLE OF CONTENTS.

DRAWN AFTER NATURE

For the Proprietor HERRMANN J. MEYER

ITASCA LAKE

THE SOURCE OF THE MISSISSIPPI RIVER

(MINNESOTA)

Published for HERRMANN J. MEYER 164 William Str. NEWYORK

LAKE ITASCA.

THE remotest source of the river Mississippi is a small horse-shoe shaped lake, known to the people of the United States by the aboriginal name Itasca. A correct view of this lake is presented in the engraving. The name Mississippi is derived from the Indian words *Missi* (great) and *se-pe* (river, or running water.) . The poetic phrase "Father of the Waters," which has gained currency, is wholly fanciful.

The most northern branches of the Mississippi have their rise in an elevated table land, abounding with marshes and lakes, with alternate ridges of sand, gravel, and erratic boulders. The swamps are generally destitute of timber, but are covered with wild rice, grass, and shrubbery. The hills abound with pines and other evergreens. During the summer, the lakes are the resort of myriads of wild fowl, which in the winter retire to a more genial climate.

Itasca Lake is surrounded with these swamps and sand ridges. Commencing in the vicinity of Leech Lake, the elevated ridges form a semi-circle around Itasca; and then stretch to the northward and northeast, dividing the waters that flow into Red River and Hudson's Bay from those that flow through the Mississippi into the Gulf of Mexico. The distance of Itasca Lake from the mouth of the Mississippi is estimated at 2896 miles, and its height above the level of the ocean at 1575 feet. Its latitude is 47° 13′ 35″, and its longitude 95° 2′ west from Greenwich.

In the month of August, the temperature of the waters was 62° while that of the atmosphere was 56° of Fahrenheit. The Mississippi River on issuing from the northern end of the Lake at that season was 16 feet wide, 14 inches in depth, and ran with a swift current. In five miles it had become enlarged to 25 feet in width, and 3 feet in depth. The portage between the south-eastern part of Itasca Lake and the extreme head of the east fork of the Mississippi is about seven miles over a spur of sand-hills, to Ossawa Lake. This Lake, which bears the same relation to the east fork as the Itasca Lake does to the main stream, is about two miles in extent, with a broad margin of aquatic plants. Its waters are dark, and abound with perch.

The Itasca fork of the river is a clear stream, with a sandy and pebbly bottom, strewed with shells, and overspread with foliage. A strong current and winding channel make its descent a work of care and danger for the frail Indian canoes which navigate its surface. The passage has to be often cleared by the axe, while every sudden bend is obstructed by piles of drift wood. Repeated series of rapids are found where the stream is compassed within narrow banks, and the water deep. Granite boulders and furious currents increase the danger.

At the distance of twelve miles, a savanna valley opens to view, and the channel grows wider and deeper, but more circuitous. This plateau extends eight or ten miles. The river then becomes narrower, and enters another series of rapids. Huge masses of rock dispute the passage, and the swift and eddying current demands the most constant exertion. Several miles below another plateau is passed over, where the Cano River enters as a tributary on the right shore. This level extends for eight or nine miles, when we reach another series of rapids, and again pass through a savanna country, with a wider and more winding channel.

The banks of the river are destitute of timber. Nothing grows along the shore but willows, a species of wild rose, and aquatic plants. On the sand ridges seen in prospective, beyond the narrow alluvion of the valley, the pine in all its varieties is the predominant tree. The willow, so common to the lower Mississippi, is seen on the first plateau, and becomes one of the constant shrubs on the savannas. The Indian reed appears a little lower down, and is associated with the wild rice. The stag and hind are the principal species of deer in these regions; the swallow-tailed hawk and the common passenger pigeon are found in abundance. A few snakes and lizards are occasionally met with, while musquitoes fill the air, and at night torment the traveller beyond endurance.

Fifty or sixty miles below Itasca, a naked bluff on the left bank of the river marks a portage leading to a lake, from which issues one of the forks of Wild Rice river, forming the commencement of the principal Indian travel to the Red River of the north. About one hundred miles down the river is the junction of the Piniddinvin, a tributary from the left, which has its origin in a lake and enters the Mississippi through an extensive marsh of wild rice, weeds, and rushes. At this stage of its progress the Mississippi widens and winds itself through the valley. In the summer months its waters are enlivened with innumerable flocks of wild fowl. After another contraction of the channel it enters Pemidje Lake, which is an expanse of the river, covering forty or fifty square miles. This lake is full of aquatic plants, with intermediate spaces of clear water which resemble channels, and make it difficult to find the true course of

the river. A few miles from this lake we come to the junction of the La Place, and enter Lake Irving. Thus far the main river has received ten tributaries.

Passing in a northerly direction, we now enter Lake Traverse, a fine sheet of water, about twelve miles long and six broad, perfectly clear and without islands. Its border is lined with gently swelling hills covered with groves of hard wood timber. To the north lies Turtle Lake, which with a series of small lakes, connected by Turtle River, forms another of the sources of the Mississippi. From the head of these waters there is a portage to Red Lake, and through that a water passage to Red River and Hudson's Bay. Turtle Lake constitutes the most northern portion of the head waters of the Mississippi. Turtle River after passing through a series of lakes enters Cass Lake on the northern side, forming a junction with the other branches of the Mississippi already noticed.

Cass Lake is an irregular body of water, about sixteen miles in extent, with four islands and several promontories. The largest of these islands is Colcaspi or Grand Isle, crowned with a forest of elm and oak. The borders of the lake are clad with elm, maple and pine, while its margin is covered with wild rice, rushes, reeds and grass. Allen's Bay is properly the head, where the Mississippi enters on the western side. On the southern shore is Pike's Bay, which presents a broad expanse of deep clear water, and a singularly picturesque prospect. This lake is about 3000 miles from the Gulf of Mexico, by the meanders of the river, and 1330 feet above the level of the Atlantic ocean at that point. It is about 100 miles from Itasca.

A portage of 450 yards leads from the south end of Pike's Bay to Moss Lake, in the bed of which are large masses of coarse fibrous moss. Through a series of lakes and a water course, a travelled route extends to Leech Lake, which forms a junction with the Mississippi, after leaving Cass Lake, and flowing through Lake Winnipec and Little Winnipec. On the borders of Leech Lake are groves of oak and sugar maple. From the last, the Indians and traders make great quantities of sugar annually. This lake is more irregular in its form than any body of water in the vast region of lakes to which it belongs. Its borders are made up of a combination of curves, points, peninsulas and bays. The margin of the lake and of its numerous bays abounds in wild rice, and at the proper season is the haunt of great quantities of water fowl. In its central parts the water is clear, from six to ten fathoms in depth, and filled with the white fish and other species. The fisheries are productive at all seasons, but are prosecuted to the best advantage in the spring and autumnal months.

The fish of the lakes, the wild rice of the bays, and the maple sugar, are the principal means of support of the Chippewas in this vicinity. Deer, elks, foxes, bears, wolverines, raccoons, weasels, and martins are found in the adjacent forests, and muskrats, minks, and a few otters in the waters. The beaver was once found in all these streams in great numbers, but through the effect of the fur-trade the race has become nearly extinct. The white-fish abounds in all the deep lakes of the upper Mississippi, and indeed in all the waters from Lake Erie to Hudson's Bay, and forms an important item in the commerce of the north-west. In Leech Lake this fish is said to be of a finer flavor than in Lake Superior, and generally weighs from seven to ten pounds. The other fish in these lakes are principally pike, pickerel, carp or sucker, perch, and a species of trout. Leech Lake swarms with leeches; and among the amphibia are several varieties of terrapin and turtle.

In 1836, an enumeration of the Indians in the vicinity of this lake made the number about one thousand souls. Their village was on what is called Otter-Tail Point. An Indian town throughout this part of North America is merely a collection of wigwams, built of small trees, and covered with bark or with mats and skins, without any regular streets or other appearances of order. An open space is left, covered with grass, where councils are held and dances performed. The plat of ground on which the village is situated, in all timbered regions, is surrounded with the native forest to protect it from the winds.

Since the year 1766, when the fur-traders entered this north-western forest, Leech Lake has been the principal post of trade. The Indians were then numerous, but the small pox and other causes have greatly reduced their numbers. They were formerly regarded as turbulent and treacherous neighbors, but they now fear the power of the United States and have become docile.

The south end of Leech Lake is in nearly the same latitude as Itasca—the river having made a vast semicircle, first north, then east, then south-east. At the junction of the lake with the main river, the course of the Mississippi is north-east, with a deep winding channel, through prairies and marshes. On the distant ridges are groves and scattering trees. The uplands are covered with white and yellow pines, spruce, fir, white cedar, birch and hemlock; the wet and low lands with the American larch and willow. On fertile portions of alluvion along the lakes, are found the sugar maple, several species of oak, ash and elm. The shrubbery consists of the wild rose and hawthorn. The wild fruits are plums, raspberries, strawberries, blackberries and cranberries. The last named fruit abounds in the swamps and marshes of Minnesota, and is gathered by the Indians for market, as it has become an article of commerce at St. Louis and other large towns on the river.

Descending from the junction of Leech River, we soon come to the river La Crose on the left, which connects with a long narrow lake of the same name. From this point to the Falls of Peckagama, about sixty miles, the river is intensely monotonous, and the voyager turns away to notice the birds and water fowl—the only evidences of life in this dreary region. The river here forms more numerous curves than in any other part of its course, winding through an extensive prairie, three miles in width, and bounded by dry sand ridges. Over these are scattered clumps of yellow pine. The rank growth of the rice, grass and rushes hides the prospect from view, and nothing is seen but the sky and this immense plain of vegetation. The width of the river here is about eighty feet, and its current does not exceed a mile in an hour.

In about thirty miles the Chevrieul or Deer River comes in from the left, and three miles further down, the Vermillion River from the right, then the channel begins to widen. Ducks, geese, and white gulls are abundant in the water, and flocks of blackbirds fill the air. Thirty-five miles further down we reach the Falls of Peckagama, where the river shoots down an inclined plane of three hundred yards and a descent of twenty feet. At this fall the Mississippi is contracted and navigation is entirely interrupted. A small rocky island at the head of the chute, covered with spruce and cedar, divides the channel in the centre. The view of the fall is quite picturesque. Here the first rock stratum is seen. Below the fall the geology of the country, the character of the river, and the productions of its borders are somewhat changed.

The country we have thus far explored is wholly of a diluvial character. Below, lime stone appears, and forests of maple, elm, oaks of various species, ash, with occasional groves of pine, diversify the scene.

At the foot of the falls the river expands with a swift current, and four miles below commence a series of rapids, which continue at intervals to Sandy Lake. There are nine distinct rapids. In addition to the birds already noticed, we find the robin, brown thrush, plover and crow. The average width of the river is about fifty yards. The only important rivers, as we pass, are Prairie, Trout and Swan rivers, which enter the Mississippi on the left.

The next point of observation is Sandy River, which is the outlet of Sandy Lake on the left. This lake is about five miles long and four broad, and lies about three miles by land from the Mississippi. It forms the most direct communication through the waters of the St. Louis River with Lake Superior. Imbedded in the ridges about Sandy Lake are masses of horne-blende, granite, argillite, sand-stone, milky and red ferruginous quartz, jasper and carnelian. The lake is of very irregular shape, indented with many bays, and pointed and studded with islands. From the early visits of the French, it has been an important post in the fur-trade, and one of the central points of Indian rendezvous on the waters of the Mississippi.

From Sandy Lake to the junction of Crow-wing River, the average breadth of the Mississippi is three hundred feet. The principal tributaries are Sable and Pine Rivers on the right. Small islands, with scanty timber now appear in the Mississippi; snags are found in its channel; and piles of drift wood that have been brought down the current in high water are lodged in its eddies. The river below begins to wash and undermine its banks, which are elevated from fifteen to twenty feet above the ordinary level of the water. Boulders of horne-blende, granite and sand-stone are in the channel.

Opposite the entrance of Crow-wing River is a large well-wooded island, which partially conceals the river from view. This river, which is in latitude 45° 49′50″ at the junction, is the largest tributary of the Mississippi above St. Peter's. By the Long

Prairie River, another principal tributary, is a route to the St. Peter's, and the avenue through which the Chippewas formerly ascended in their war-path against their ancient enemies the Sioux. Many traditions are related of adventures on this stream, or the adjacent plains. The land on the borders of Crow-wing River is fertile, and covered with a heavy growth of elm, sugar-maple, black-walnut and oak.

Several miles below Crow-wing island, at the entrance of the Nokay, is Fort Gaines, intended to protect the advancing American population, and to control the scattered Indian tribes above. Civilization is making rapid strides towards this point. A small steamboat was launched above the Falls of St. Anthony in the spring of 1850, which made regular trips to the Sauh Rapids, to which point settlements have been formed along the eastern shore.

The Buffalo Plains commence here, and extend on both sides of the Mississippi to the Falls of St. Anthony. The face of the country is undulating, and the prairies alternate with groves of shrubby oaks. Occasionally high promontories extend from the bank of the river and form romantic cliffs; but generally the banks on both sides have an elevation of not more than fifteen or twenty feet. The whole country from Crow-wing River to the falls, is favorable to agriculture. The timber on the western shore is abundant, and of good quality, consisting of oak, elm, ash, sugar maple and swamp maple, hickory, birch, and other trees. The soil is a mixture of sand, gravel and clay. Small rivers skirted with timber meander through the prairies, and beautiful pellucid lakes embellish the scenery.

At several points below Fort Gaines, there are shoals and rapids in the river, but the principal obstruction consists in erratic boulders, which may be removed at small expense; a work which has been commenced in the action of the territorial government of Minnesota.

The only tributaries for some distance are Elk and Sauh Rivers on the right, and St. Francis of Hennepin and Carver on the left, which is the highest point reached by either of the first European explorers. About fifteen miles above the Falls of St. Anthony, is Mississawgaigan or Rum River, which has its origin in Spirit Lake, at a great distance in the north-east.

The whole country which we have described is included in the territory of Minnesota. This territory was organized on the first of June, 1849, by the Hon. Alexander Ramsay, who was the first Governor appointed by the President of the United States. Its name is derived from the aboriginal name of St. Peter's—*minne*, running water, and *sota*, muddy or rather slightly turbid. The climate of this region in summer and autumn is dry and sultry; in winter the whole country is covered with ice and snow. The atmosphere is purified by frequent winds, and the temperature is usually favorable to health. This territory embraces an area of 166,000 square miles, and in a few years will doubtless procure the requisite population for one or more new States of the American Union.

FALLS OF ST. ANTHONY.

As we approach the Falls of St. Anthony from Rum River, the bed of the Mississippi is almost one continuous series of rapids, with eddies and pools, formed by the winding channel. On both sides are undulating prairies, interspersed with small groves and strips of shrubby oak. Above the Falls, the river has formed a long narrow island, extending towards the left bank. Another small island, immediately below divides the cataract into two unequal sheets of water, which pour over a ledge of limestone rock, with a perpendicular pitch of 16½ feet. The whole descent above and below the cataract, within the limits of the portage, is about 60 feet.

The best point of observation is on the eastern shore. Above the cataract, the river is 600 yards wide, while below it is only about 200. The craggy and rocky banks are steep, and a chain of high bluffs intercepts the horizon. A mill-dam has recently been constructed across the eastern channel, forming an immense water-power, on which a large lumber-mill is in operation above the Little Falls. Between the long island and the eastern shore the aspect of nature has been changed by the still water of the mill-pond, which is covered with immense drifts of pine logs, floated down from the upper forests, and lodged in this harbor until converted into lumber.

Below the cataract are huge masses of rock, broken from the ledge of limestone over which the water pours, as the sandstone foundation on which it rests is washed away. On the brow of the falls, rough and pointed gray rocks emerge from the flood, behind which, at a low stage of water, lie large trees, brush roots and weeds, which have been arrested on their career down the river. The water, on escaping from the precipice, rushes downwards, boiling, foaming and tumbling over its rocky bed; the strong current lashing the obstructions on the surface, or hissing in a wild whirlpool, it writhes in a thousand contortions, until it passes the rocky channel half a mile below, and assumes its calm and placid course.

The beautiful Cataract Island which divides the main cataract from Little Falls, as the eastern chute is called, gladdens the eye of the traveller with the freshness and abundance of its vegetation. Oak, spruce, hemlock, and occasional evergreens are interlaced with the wild grape, hazel, and bramble bush. Long Island and Cataract Island were formerly the rendezvous of eagles and other birds of prey. The vast quantities of fish with which the pools and eddies abound, as well as those which are dashed in pieces in descending the falls and washed on shore, furnished plentiful supplies of food for their young—but the bustle of civilization has now driven them away.

The Little Falls are about 130 yards in width. When viewed from one of the huge slabs of rock piled up in the channel below, the scenery presents a singularly grand and picturesque appearance. The ragged outline of the brink of the Falls—the tall green forest of Cataract Island—the lofty cliffs of the opposite banks of the river—the light blue North American sky stretched out over the landscape—give an aspect of romantic beauty to the scene, which is rarely equalled amid the indescribable enchantments of nature. The Dacotah Indians in their expressive language call this place Minne-ra-ra, "the water that laughs."

The approach to the main cataract on ascending the river, presents little of the grandeur and sublimity which characterize the view of Niagara Falls from the gulf below. We do not hear that deep and appalling roar of the waters, nor feel the tremulous motion of the rocks under our feet, which impress the mind of the beholder with a sense of majesty and awe. But the Falls of St. Anthony have a charm of their own in their simple beauty and their harmonious blending of the wild and the picturesque. They are more cheerful and exhilarating, if less sublime and overwhelming.

When the river is at its greatest height, the aspect of the Falls is somewhat changed, and exhibits more magnificent and impressive features. The increased volume of water rushing with new velocity over the rocky precipice, throws off a spray, from which, in clear weather, all the hues of the rainbow are reflected; and when the sky is overcast, this spray forms a dense cloud which covers the place with gloom, inspiring the soul with feelings of solemn awe.

The Falls of St. Anthony form a transition point in the geology of the country. The primitive rock is no longer seen in *situ*, but only appears in errratic boulders, scattered over the face of the country towards the south, and extending to the lower parts of Illinois and Missouri. The beautiful prairies above, which are often found on the margin of the river, are merged in the rugged lime-stone cliffs that skirt its bank, and the alluvial bottoms that prevail from that point downwards. Above the Falls, the prairies do not consist of an unbroken plain, but are diversified with hills and vales, covered with grass and flowers, and interspersed with groves of oak, which give beauty and animation to the scene.

The first European who visited and described these falls, was Father Louis Hennepin, a companion, for a time, of La Salle. He gave them the name which they now bear, in honor of his patron, St. Anthony of Padua. A party to explore the "Great River" towards its source was arranged by La Salle, while he returned from Illinois to Fort Frontinac to prepare for an expedition down the same stream. Leaving Fort Creve-Cœur on the Illinois river, on the last day of February, 1680, Father Hennepin with his party, reached the Mississippi which was full of floating ice, in seven days. They made the best of their way up the icy stream, and on the 11th of April were at Rock Island. Here the whole party were taken prisoners by a band of Dacotah Indians. Each of the Frenchmen was adopted into one of the Indian families, and was treated with kindness. They then proceeded further up the Mississippi, and towards the last of July, Siéur de Luth, with five Canadians, arrived at the Indian camp on a trading expedition. Hennepin joined the party, ascended the river to the Falls, and proceeding to St. Francis, returned with de Luth to Canada, and afterwards to France, where he published his "Discovery of Louisiana."

The first English colonist who visited the cataract, was Captain Jonathan Carver. This took place in November, 1766. He too reached the St. Francis river, and passed the winter with the Dacotahs.

A town named "The City of the Falls of St. Anthony" has been laid out on the eastern side of the river opposite the Little Falls, which has already become a respectable village. It is situated on an elevated prairie, with a gentle ascent from the water, and a tract of table land in the rear, thirty feet above the level of the stream.

Below the Falls, the bed of the river, which is contracted to about 200 yards in width, extends through a deep ravine between lofty cliffs, seven miles to St. Paul, making a descent in this distance of about eighty feet.

SAN FRANCISCO.

The history of the world presents both in ancient and modern times, some examples of cities rapidly built and peopled. But these are rare, the growth of such communities being, as a general rule, slow. The power of particular princes or dictators, rising to despotism, has enabled them occasionally, by means of centralization, to stimulate certain cities into rapid increase; but this has been done uniformly at the expense of other portions of the empire. We read of Sennacherib building Babylon; which means simply, that the rest of the empire was suddenly deprived of much of its resources, to exaggerate one imperial point. So, too, the building of Alexandria by the great conqueror, was simply a kingly fiat, and not a necessity of increasing wealth, admitting even the sagacity which chose such a spot as a commercial entrepot for the purpose of conducting the traffic with the east, then first permitted by the destruction of the Persian empire. Cæsar boasted that he found Rome built of brick and left it of marble; a boast which shadowed forth the destruction of the empire, as it caused the provinces to sustain the idle and ferocious rabble who centred there, and increased involuntary labor in the ratio of the degradation of all industry. The formation of Venice was an industrial protest against barbaric irruption, and the duration and power of that city, though belonging to a small state, and notwithstanding the aristocratic element of its government, for so long a period, was due to the economy of its origin. M. Thiers attributes the wealth and power of Venice to the aristocratic element, but the truth is that they grew in spite of it, and not in virtue of it. The supremacy of Paris is not owing to the natural advantages of the place, but to centralization, and its predominance has been at the cost of the empire and of periodical revolutions. The colonial system, and the manufacturing and commercial greed of Great Britain, have given London her preponderance; otherwise we should not see twenty-four hundred thousand people squeezed together out of a population of less than thirty millions. Of all the rapid growths of cities in the United States, during the last century, none equalled Philadelphia, because of its mild government and comparatively favorable position for markets and political congresses, and the peculiarly good auspices of its foundation. Since the opening of the Erie Canal, the improvements in ship building, and the navigation of the ocean by steam, the increment of the city of New York has been wonderfully great. During the last forty years the city alone has augmented in

DRAWN AFTER NATURE

For the Proprietor: HERRMANN J. MEYER.

SAN FRANCISCO

Published for HERRMANN J. MEYER. 164, William-Str. NEWYORK.

numbers as much as England did in the same period a century ago. This growth however, has not been without some of the evils of centralization, as the state at large must be impoverished by a system which causes so great a portion of her products to be eaten away from the spots where they are raised. The growth of Cincinnati is marvellous; a large city already, and within the memory of a distinguished inhabitant, Judge Burnet, who died the other day, it was composed of less than a score of log huts. Other towns of the west, are hardly, if at all, less remarkable than Cincinnati for rapid growth.

Of all the communities which indicate a quick rise, however, Californian San Francisco affords the most signal example. The Hindoo jugglers have the secret of making lettuce grow in a few minutes. The necromancers of California do more, they make a city grow in a few days. It is almost a paradoxical term to say that San Francisco grew. It was extemporized. By a series of circumstances a war was most unexpectedly engendered between the United States and Mexico; for among prescient statesmen, so called of a certain period, we look in vain for any prophecy respecting it, and it was the last thing to be desired. This war resulted in the acquisition of California, and a third accident was the discovery of GOLD. Philosophy and religion join in denouncing the lust of wealth, but never were their voices more impotent in staying the tide of adventure in quest of it, than when the astounding fact was announced that the newly acquired territory was auriferous, that the precious dust could be had for the digging, and that the career of fortune lay broadly open to all. Never in the history of the world were the accessories to such colonization so free. There were no adverse deities as in ancient times to propitiate; no augurs to consult as to prospects, with the reserved theological privilege of putting off the expedition, *sine die.* Nor was there a court or clergy as in the middle ages, to win or wheedle before a few thirty ton vessels could be fitted out. And when ready, there were no cowardly crews dreading Olympian thunders, saintly frowns, or flying Dutchmen. None of these moral impediments, while our material superiority over olden times was equally marked. For the wooden walls of Old England were overtopped, her swiftest craft outsped, in the vessels and steamers that flew over the ocean. Never, never, in all the annals of this globe were such nautical powers exhibited. Big, fearful distances dissolved under the press of sail or force of steam. Short isthmus cuts were discovered. Overland routes, with Mormondom as a half way, were opened. Speculation shone in commercial eyes; from machine-sawed timber to bottles of soda-water, from ready-made metal houses to ready-made metal coffins,—food, raiment, shelter,—all were shipped to the golden coast. New York suddenly seemed turned into a Californian Commissariat. The interest of European revolutions hung fire. Socialistic heroes were at a discount. Court twaddle and heraldic fanfaronade wanted readers this side the water. The maxims of Poor Richard were less heard of than ever. The return cargoes, the personal news from California electrified the public. How many a heart beat with a whir of throbs, how many an eye rained with tears, as letter on letter came from the mines—the first written, perhaps the last! How the newspapers had a new branch of industry, in detailing the Pacific gold fever and its train of excitements—its frenzied industry—its blasting dangers—its hurry, rush, ecstacy—its chivalric encounters—its wild tragedies—a nonpareil community whether in the story of life or death. For here the people were before the government. No hierarchy, spiritual or temporal guarded them. Neither benedictions nor bayonets kept them in order. Each man for himself, with the instinct for the public good determining without effort laws necessary for the preservation of the community at large. While Congress was hesitating to form a government except on certain conditions, for the new territory, it made one of its own. Trained lawyers, legislators, and editors were not there for nothing. They could handle the pickaxe, carry loads, do any kind of mental labour, and did it to the wonderment of Europe. Bound down with caste; overridden with hereditary pomposity; steeped in poverty, owing to the idea, that certain professions, chiefly arms, alone are respectable, and that he who digs, hammers, sews, cooks, carries or drives, is no peer of the harlequin soldier, luckily born land-owner, the bloated money-king, Europe stared, wondered, laughed and set up lotteries out of the ingots for those who were too proud and dishonest to go work for them.

The laws of California were benign. Come all those who are lightly laden and try to get gold. France, although by her laws no one can dig the mines on his own estate at home, did not fail to send out a troublesome set of braves to seek their fortunes in our placer. Germany, England, all lent a hand to the diggings. Even stand-still China afforded us an extract of her sons, and California became the speculating maelstrom of the world. Under these influences, of course, the subject of our notice, San Francisco was extemporized. We have before us in Bayard Taylor's *El Dorado*, a picture of San Francisco in November, 1848. It numbers, all told, less than thirty houses, with shipping to match. One year afterwards, a city was painted with a forest of masts, under the same title. Under such magical growth, the nature of speculations may be well imagined. Land that a few months before might have been had almost for the asking, was sold at metropolitan prices. The rates of living were paid for in gold, and at fabulous price. "The great want of San Francisco," says Mr. Taylor, "was society. Think of a city of thirty thousand inhabitants peopled by men alone! The like of this was never seen before. Every man was his own housekeeper, doing in many instances, his own sweeping, washing, and mending. Many home arts, learned rather by observation than experience, came conveniently into play. He who cannot make a bed, cook a beef steak, sew up his own rips and rents, is unfit to be a citizen of California. Nevertheless, since the town began to assume a permanent shape, very many of the comforts of life in the East were attainable." Since that author wrote, the condition of San Francisco has become metropolitan. Society does exist. Women have come to the rescue. Side-walks are paved for their promenades. The city has taken definite shape. In view of its immense future, we trust the errors of the Atlantic cities will be avoided, as to plan; that economies suited to the climate may be adopted, especially in devoting a thousand or two acres to the purposes of public gardens and parks, the cheapest and best of common investments.

The physiology of San Francisco is of course American. It is remarkable that the immigrants of whatever country in Europe, English, Dutch, French, Spanish, simply transferred the shape and style of houses and streets, (less gardens and parks,) of their several countries to the colonies, never attempting any novelty to suit a new climate. In this not a ray of genius was discovered, but stupid iteration and dismal commonplace. Some bold innovator might strike out something new for the city of the Pacific, which would illustrate the genius of the people, and meet the peculiarities of the climate. Why could not each street have an alley of trees, making a very tunnel of verdure, and defying the scorching rays of the sun? Why cannot art take a religious aspect, and God make the town as well as the country?

In 1845 San Francisco had but one hundred and fifty inhabitants. In April, 1847, there were three hundred and seventy-five, besides a few Indians. In October, 1847, there were eight hundred. In October, 1848, one hundred and fifty votes were polled; and December, 1848, three hundred and forty-seven. In August, 1849, there were 1,519 votes cast. In January, 1853, the city contained 30,000 people, and about 10,000 voters. In March, 1847, there were only six vessels in port; and on the 18th of the following December, only four, and no arrival for a week. In January, February and March, of 1848, there were but nine arrivals, four of which were from the neighboring ports of Monterey and San Pedro; and for the last quarter of 1847, the imports amounted to $49,00, and the exports to $63,600. From the 1st of January, to the 31st of October, 1852, the duties received at the Custom House amounted to $1,560,842 15, and the number of passengers arriving by sea during the same period, was 58,851, while those who departed in the same manner were 19,575. The first brick building was erected in September, 1848, and this was the second brick house in Upper California, there being one at that date in Monterey. In the first two months after the discovery of gold, in December, 1847, the amount of dust brought to San Francisco was about $250,000, and during the next two months about $600,000. Now it is five millions a month. The first Protestant house of worship in California was built by the Baptists, and was dedicated on the 5th of August, 1849. At the present time there are eighteen churches, two of which are Catholic, and the rest Protestant. January 1, 1853, there were five daily and seven weekly newspapers; twenty private banking houses; twenty-four auction houses; four bath houses; sixteen bakeries; seventeen barber shops; forty-two blacksmiths; nine booksellers and stationers; thirty-three boot and shoe dealers; twenty-eight butchers; fifty-nine master carpenters and builders; sixty-two clothiers; nine dealers in crockery and glass-ware; one hundred and thirty commission merchants; twenty-eight dry-goods dealers; thirty-four druggists; nine furniture dealers; nine fancy dry-goods; twenty-seven hardware dealers; ninety-three groceries; six livery stables; twenty-six milliner and dress-makers' shops; twenty-two house and sign painters; eight saddle and harness makers; nine ship chandlers; twenty-four stove and tin-ware dealers; twenty-three tailor shops; eighteen upholsterers; forty dealers in watches and jewelry; about sixty physicians; and about one hundred and fifty lawyers.

As the prosperity of San Francisco depends on that of the State of California at large, the following mention of the wealth and resources of the latter may be well introduced here:—

In two years the population has increased thirty per cent., and it is thought that in ten years it will have at least quadrupled. There are, as at present estimated, 308,000 inhabitants, the annual increase being thirty-nine per cent. greater than that of the other States. If this augmentation continue, it is not difficult to prophesy the formation of a great empire on the Pacific in a very short space of time, composed of a population singularly varied in its elements, and stimulated, without gold mines even, to the successful industry peculiar to our institutions.

The estimated value of capital employed in agriculture, real estate and improvements, is as follows:

Capital employed in stock, farming, and gardening,	$1,857,502	Agricultural products,	$6,162,040
Do. in fruits and orchards,	366,910	Land in cultivation,	1,207,480
Do. in improvements and real estate,	6,348,346	Estimate of El Dorado and Calaveras,	5,000,000
Do. farming utensils,	125,940	Horticulture, manufactures, &c.,	1,150,000
Do. milling,	240,850	Quartz mining,	5,871,405
Estimate of El Dorado and Calaveras Co.'s,	10,000,000	Placer,	4,174,419
Live stock,	18,903,714	Others,	3,851,623
		Estimate for El Dorado mining,	2,500,000
Total,			$108,522,568

In the above estimate no land except that in actual cultivation is included.

The comparative agricultural wealth of California thus appears:

In horses she is in advance of fifteen of the States; in mules, of twenty-six States; milch cows, of twelve States; in working oxen, of eight; in value of live stock of twenty States; in barley she is only equalled by New York; in potatoes next to New York, and yields more than one-half of all produced in the Union; wheat greater than ten of the States; in oats, she exceeds three-fourths of the other States; in hay, exceeding nine of the States; in mining, without a parallel; in fruits, exceeding all the States in variety, and one-half of them in quantity produced.

Such are the wonderful city and country of the Pacific. Nurtured up to this time chiefly by the industry and enterprise of the East, California may begin soon, however, to take upon itself an indigenous strength, contributing to the common glory and grandeur of our vast empire. That it must form one destiny with ourselves, is now determined; and to abolish the excess of distance, and identify the interests of the Pacific coast with the Atlantic, it will be necessary to construct without delay a RAILROAD from the Mississippi to SAN FRANCISCO.

NEW ORLEANS

Published for HERRMANN J.MEYER. 8. North William-Street. NEWYORK.

NEW ORLEANS.

Not quite a hundred miles from the meeting of the Mississippi's turbid flood with the uncertain billows of the Mexican Gulf, is situated New Orleans—the Crescent City. Crescent in the shape of its water front, and crescent in its advance and prosperity. Not quite a hundred miles from the union of river water and gulf waves, where advanced the prow of La Salle, the discoverer, one hundred and seventy-one years ago, to enable that gallant voyager to take possession of land "in the name of the most puissant, most holy, most invincible and victorious Prince Louis, the Great King of France."

Forty years afterwards came Bienville to found the city which he named after the race of Dukes, whom many loyal hearts in *la belle France* deem not yet extinct from the hope of sovereign rule—an event which if it ever comes let us wish may find a policy of king-government in name like our subject—indeed a *new* Orleans. Bienville the younger brother and best beloved of Iberville, whose policy did so much for the benefit of Louisiana, was not unfortunate in the selection of his city-site. If it was distant from the sea, it was bounded upon all sides by the water—and in more directions than one a port of entry. To the lakes, at the rear of the city, came the name of the noble Count Ponchartrain, one of the best chancellors of France, in the days when chancellors were most needed; and of his grandson, Count Maurepas, whose political greatness is not to be lightly despised by the muse of History. Thousands are borne upon Lakes Ponchartrain and Maurepas, who never think of the age which gave them names, or of the romance which once came to their shores as the freight of ships from a dissolute and voluptuous court. Puritan Plymouth, and Burgher New York, and chivalric Baltimore, and struggling Jamestown, and (all along the Southern coast to which the Huguenots came, or such adventurous souls as Ponce de Leon) the islands which are so like

> "Moles that dot the dimpled bosom
> Of the sunny summer sea,"

each preserve with the chronicler their legends of fascination, but New Orleans, true to the time of its origin, contains the wildest and most voluptuous romance. Were not Manon Lescaut, Chevalier D'Aubant, the Princess Charlotte of Brunswick, Wolfenbüttel, the buried, yet not dead wife of Alexis Petrowitz, (that wayward monster of a noble Czar,) and Bellisle, and John Law, each connected with its early reminiscences? And not in the most comprehensive collections of fiction, will be found more exciting detail than is drawn up from the wells of historical truth by one of New Orleans' most favored sons—Charles Gayarre, whose history in French, and lectures in English, are found upon the shelves of every well assorted American library.

New Orleans was thoroughly French in its origin, and French in its progress. Not until the Saxon spade came to turn its thin soil, and the Saxon mind to direct its destinies, did the city take those rapid steps which made her so quickly a Metropolis of the South. Yet the endeavors and hopes and toils of the early French settlers and governors are never to be despised; according to their light and judgment did they work; but theirs was not the great labor for posterity. But there have been few Frenchmen who ever paid court to any other offspring of time than "the present." New Orleans had its days of partizan struggle. Spanish dominion and French rule quarrelled for supremacy over its narrow belt of land. That was a wise foresight of Napoleon to sell what he could no longer keep, and of President Jefferson to purchase what other nations might well desire to conquer away from American possession. Yet the purchase of Louisiana evoked the anathemas of French pride and American caution, in times when the party of "progress" had not yet organized nor flung out tauntingly upon the breeze its purple flag.

It is not difficult, even to-day, in walking through the early built portion of New Orleans, to conjure up all the associations of its origin. Every street has its original name taken from Dukes, and Princes, and places esteemed the most by the immigrants from France. Low roofed houses whisper of Spanish builders; and narrow streets and balconies, and arched carriageways, pronounce the Parisian architect's name. Long was the struggle for the city's government between French or Creole and American genius. But Saxon policy has prevailed in all its issues. Once there were three Municipalities, and all the suburbs were called Faubourgs, as in the Gallic cities, which the founders emulated. But Americans three years ago inscribed upon municipal banners the word consolidation, and then in place of double rulers, and treble policies, and sectional improvements, New Orleans became a whole, and again strided on with prosperous opportunities.

The city is difficult to describe, and difficult to write about. It must be seen to be known; so different are its complexion and ways from the other American cities. From the river Mississippi to Lake Ponchartrain, it has a gentle descent of some half a dozen miles. Commencing on the bank of the former with a levee or dyke, and ending towards the latter in a swamp, which the Creole ruler thought impassable, but from which American engineers are driving the miasma and gases of disease, to make room for the store houses, that at no very distant day will astonish the placid waters of the Lake by their shadows,—the water front of the city curves inward like a half moon, and far away to the Gulf the shore still goes on in a tortuous course. The levee or dyke, which protects the city from inundation when the spring waters swell the river current, serves as wharf also. And being broad and wide of reach, its surface is made to tremble with the weight of the tobacco, the cotton, and the sugar of domestic export. The city stretches along the river for four or five miles, but is scarcely a mile in compact depth towards the lake. The first built section of the city may be said to form a mile square, and is thickly studded with buildings. It may be recognized from the river by the absence of steeples. The younger portion of the metropolis (as in the cut before us) shows the steeples, which are always raised where Saxon architects go. The stores affect the localities nearest to the river. Take these away from New Orleans and one half its compactness is gone. The steamboats receive attention in the midway portion of the levee front, and the fleets of ships are the extreme wings.

A very noisy, bustling and interesting place is that Levee. Whether at early morning you walk over its extent, from the Ponchartrain depot to the cotton presses, by its upper end, and weary your brain with counting the boxes, and bales and hogsheads about. Or whether at high business tide you stand bewildered with the clamors of sailors, and stevedores and draymen; or by the entanglement of mules and steamboat hands who are the concomitants of an arrival or a departure by the river side. Or whether, toward the evening, you listen to the ringing of steamboat bells, or watch the heavy smoke obscure the brilliancy of the sun-set. All is far different from the commercial bustle of Boston, New York, or Philadelphia, where only a few are in a hurry. In New Orleans every body is in a hurry, and the hurry all reaches a climax by the river side, where the view is far extending. Trade in the former cities is a moving panorama which you behold in parts and at intervals. In New Orleans it is a mammoth picture which you may survey at a glance.

The streets are quite straight and stretch over a thin layer of soil which the laborer's spade, at three or four feet through, breaks into water. The foundations of high buildings are rather broad than deep, and cellars are unknown. Shade trees abound, and might be more cultivated if the shop-keepers were not so proud of their signs. There are few trees more beautiful than the catalpa—*l'arbre d'amour*. (For as the story goes, the romantic young French settler yearning for something to love, who swore to wed the first woman who arrived from France, conducted beneath this tree the subject of his oath, and there confided to her its purport. He became, of course, an accepted lover, and the tree was rightly named *l'arbre d'amour*. For, although the offer may have been no compliment under the circumstances, French girls, in those days, left the saloons of Paris for New Orleans, and—a husband as the ships in returning cleared for Havre and a—market.)

The markets of New Orleans, if not so profusely supplied as those of New York, or so cleanly and prime as those of Philadelphia, are certainly better lounging places by reason of the novelties. The negro hucksters and negresses have a way of their own in dispensing their wares, and they transact business in the primitive currency which ignores cents as barbarous *bakscheesh*, and converts sixpence into "picayune," and shilling into a "bit."

The hotels and restaurants of New Orleans are inimitable for comfort, attention and good living. The hotels, St. Charles, St. Louis, and the Verandah are the ones most resorted to. The former opened in the winter of 1853, for the second time; the first erection having been destroyed by fire two years previously. And it is quite a traveller's study—that hotel life in New Orleans—through the winter—so motley are the groups—so diverse the manners—and so peculiar the different tastes of the lodgers.

The first amusement of the New Orleans populace is business, and after that come the ordinary pleasures of the metropolis. But if its theatricals and operas are more brilliant than its lecturers and lyceums, or its soirees more sought after than its conversaziones, you may find the reason in that absence of repose, and demand for excitement which are as peculiar to New Orleans as its soil.

It was once the capital of Louisiana and should yet be, instead of Baton Rogue, but the simple fellows from the interior were afraid of the virtue of their members, which were sometimes said to fall before the suppers and blandishments of the city lobbyists. There was some talk, too, of yellow fever. But that is undoubtedly a bug-bear of the past. That epidemic to the Crescent City, now the engineers have taken the swamp in hand, is something as historical as the the battle of New Orleans.

The battle ground is some five miles below the city—a league or so before you strike with your eye a certain course of the river yet called "English Turn." For, as every creole urchin in the city learns at school, it was at this locality an English gun frigate, ascending the river on an exploration, encountered Monsieur Iberville going down. The Englishmen was informed that the French had been a long time in possession, and had founded settlements, and so, not deigning to inquire into the truth of the settlements, or to debate the superior right of the French, he turned back and went to sea. Hence the name *le detour aux Anglais*—"the English turn." The battle ground is, however, little marked. The localities of movement are yet pointed out by the keen eyes of veterans who were present at the engagement, but smiling sugar fields for the most part occupy "*the plains of Chalmette.*"

To New Orleans, of course, hasten the freights of St. Louis, Cincinnati, Louisville, and all the cities of the Missouri, Mississippi, Ohio, Red and other tributary rivers. There is no moment of the day, at any place upon the main river, where the ear can fail to hear the noise of the ascending or descending boats. Some with their two or three thousand bales of cotton—like huge floating warehouses—others with hides, tobacco, grain, flax, hemp, bagging and sugar. And thus the Crescent City becomes the factor for a country nearly as large as Europe. Of years past the western and eastern men have raged a pertinacious war upon her facilities, by their far reaching railways—and to some extent, perhaps, have tapped her trade. But the endeavor was only an incentive, and soon Mississippi wilds, in example of the Hudson Highlands, will listen hourly to the whistle of the locomotive. The railroad system for New Orleans will make her future doubly prosperous, and the only wonder is, that her citizens should have been so long in making the discovery.

New Orleans is not a religious place, but its public and private morality will favorably compare with even New England cities. It may have its operas and plays, and balls of Sabbath evenings, but its race of street rowdies, its nightly robberies and stabbings, its outrages upon delicate and undefended women, its lawless defies of the police, its aldermanic harpies are almost entirely unknown. And yet in this respect the most erroneous ideas prevail through the whole land. Fictions of the pistol, the bowie-knife, and the lonely suburb are vividly living in many a country village, to whose inhabitants a departure for New Orleans is second only to an emigration into the jungles of India.

To the traveller whose patriotism leads him to view "the United States illustrated," by the hand of actual nature, and the works of living art, no city more invites him than New Orleans. Through its foreign origin; through its complex associations of society; through its bustle of trade and excitement of amusement; through its well ordered hotels; through its thirst for progress; and through its destiny in the future.

THE PRAIRIE.

The traveller standing upon the edge of one of our large western prairies, for the first time, casts his eye over the vast expanse, with a deep feeling of astonishment. A level plain of verdure, without a single tree or shrub, or other object, to break the continuity of the prospect, stretches off in the distance, until it meets the horizon. Upon these silent wastes, a sense of utter solitude oppresses the lonely traveller. He sees nothing but the blue sky over his head, and the wide plain beneath his feet. Proceeding mile after mile, and hour after hour, he finds the same solemn monotony, perhaps occasionally interrupted by a herd of deer quietly grazing on their native domain. At length, a faint cloud is seen on the edge of the horizon; this looms higher and higher in the sky, till the long line of forest that skirts the prairie, becomes distinctly visible.

It is only in its wild uncultivated state, that the prairie is seen in all its beauty and lonely grandeur. When divided into farms, its deep silence is broken by the sounds of busy life, and it loses all traces of the peculiar character, which distinguishes it from other champaign regions. Every season of the year, almost every month, changes the features of the prairie. In the spring and summer, flowers of every hue are mingled with the tall grass that gently bends to the breeze, bearing no slight resemblance to the bosom of the ocean, when its waves are faintly moved. Different species of flowers spring up in succession, each giving a different color to the landscape. A variety of the helianthus, known among the early settlers by the name of "rosin weed," from a resinous matter that exudes from the joints of the stalk, bears a bright yellow blossom which always inclines to the sun. This is succeeded by a purple flower, and that by one of another hue, and so on in endless profusion, until vegetation is touched by the frost.

DRAWN AFTER NATURE

For the Proprietor: HERRMANN J. MEYER

PRAIRIE NEAR THE ARKANSAS-RIVER

Published for HERRMANN J. MEYER. 164, William Str. NEW YORK.

In the latter part of autumn, when the grass has become withered and dry, a slight wreath of smoke ascends from the prairie, at the distance, perhaps, of several miles from the observer. At first, it appears no larger than that which arises from the chimney of a settler's cabin; in a few moments it has increased in size; a breeze springs up, and the flames wildly career over the prairie. Volumes of smoke roll up to the heavens, and the fire rushes on with new violence. As night falls upon the scene, the conflagration is beheld in all its terrific grandeur. The whole region, for many miles, is lighted up with the glare of the burning fuel. The cattle, with the instinct of self-preservation, rush to their homes on the borders of the forest, and stand among the trees gazing with terror upon the scene. Scattered near the woodlands are the rough cabins of the pioneers, towards which the devouring flames are moving fiercely. Every inmate able to carry a brand of fire is now aroused, and takes his station along the line of furrows previously turned on the side facing the open prairie. A succession of "back fires" are now kindled up wherever there is a field or a cabin exposed. These rush forward over the dry grass until flame meets flame, and there die away for want of further material. If the unlucky farmer is absent, or has neglected to plough around his fields in early summer, his fences, and often his dwelling and wheat-stacks, become the prey of the resistless conflagration. Occasionally these fires sweep over the farms adjoining the prairie, in spite of the efforts of the watchful owner. Loss of life some times occurs, when an inexperienced person is panic-struck at the approaching fire.

"In the winter," says Judge Hall, "the prairies present a gloomy and desolate scene. The fire has passed over them and consumed every vegetable substance, leaving the soil bare and the surface perfectly black. That graceful waving outline, which was so attractive to the eye when clad in green, is now disrobed of all its ornaments, its fragrance, its notes of joy, and the graces of its landscape have all vanished, and the bosom of the cold earth, scorched and discolored, is alone visible. The wind sighs mournfully over the black plain; but there is no object to be moved by its influence—not a tree to wave its long arms in the blast, nor a reed to bend its fragile stem—not a leaf, nor even a blade of grass to tremble in the breeze. There is nothing to be seen but the cold and dead earth, and the bare mound, which move not—and the traveller with a singular sensation, almost of awe, feels the blast rushing over him, while not an object, visible to the eye, is seen to stir. Accustomed as the mind is to associate with the wind, its operation upon surrounding objects, and to see nature bowing and trembling, and the fragments of matter mounting upon the wind, as the storm passes, there is a novel effect produced on the mind of one who feels the current of air rolling heavily over him, while nothing moves around."

The country bordering on the Mississippi river, in its superficial aspect, has three natural divisions. There are forest lands, barrens (called in Michigan and Wisconsin oak openings), and prairies. Forest or timber land is too well-known to require description. "Barren" is a provincial term, denoting an intermediate condition between forest and prairie. In the early settlements of Kentucky, large tracts of country were found south of Green River, covered with scattered stunted forest trees, intermixed with hazel and other shrubs, and producing a luxuriant growth of prairie grass. From its appearance the explorers supposed the soil to be unsuitable for cultivation, and called these tracts "barren," a term now applied extensively in the west to similar tracts. The soil, though not as deep as in the rich prairies, or alluvial forests, is very productive. It is on these tracts, that the contest between the autumnal fires and the timber is kept up, until, in the progress of settlement, the fires are stopped, when the timber grows with astonishing rapidity, and the land improves in quality.

The English term "meadow" expresses the characteristic meaning of the French word "prairie," for it is used to describe every kind of land that is destitute of timber and brushwood, and clothed with grass. Moist, dry, level, undulating, are terms of description merely, and apply to prairies in the same sense as they do to forests. South of the forty second degree of north latitude, and near the Mississippi, the timber is found along the stream. Often, however, the prairies extend on the alluvial bottom to the very margin of the great river. The border of the prairie are by no means uniform. Large points of timber project into the prairie, and line the banks of the river and smaller streams, while, between these streams, points of prairie extend into the forest. Coppices and groves of forest trees, of every variety of size and shape, appear at intervals in the large prairies, like islands in the ocean. Wisconsin, Iowa, and Southern Illinois abound with such groves.

The prairies, which we have described, are rarely level. They often appear so to the eye of the stranger, but more careful observation, especially with the instrument of the engineer, detects the fallacy. The prairie which exhibits the strongest resemblance to a plain, is undulating and quickly throws off the surface water, after the fall of great quantities of rain. Generally on the upper Mississippi, from the Falls of St. Anthony to the mouth of the Des Moines, the prairies are very undulating, with elevated ridges from three to five hundred feet above the water-courses.

DRAWN AFTER NATURE

For the Proprietor: HERRMANN J. MEYER.

FORT SNELLING

(MINNESOTA)

Published for HERRMANN J. MEYER. 164. William-Street. NEWYORK.

FORT SNELLING.

THE scenery around Fort Snelling, which is situated on a high limestone bluff, near the confluence of the St. Peter's with the Mississippi river, is of a sublime and impressive character. Huge slabs of rock in the bed of the river, and the towering cliffs on either side, reveal the existence of a mighty cataract, in a remote age of the world, of which the receding Falls of St. Anthony now present only the diminished remains.

About fifty years ago, an Indian camp stood on the bluff, now occupied by Fort Snelling; bare-headed squaws, in deer-skin garments, with papooses cradled on their backs, were paddling their light bark canoes across the river; some were dressing the skins of the game, which their dusky lords had killed; while in the silence of the night, the shriek of the faithful wife was often heard under the scaffold on which was placed the dead body of her husband. The Indian braves, decked out with eagle-feathers and other warlike ornaments, held their riotous carouse, feasting on venison and dog-meat, and making the forest resound with their hideous melodies. At other times, the neighboring cliffs re-echoed with the war-whoop; the streams were stained with the blood of the Chippewas and Sioux, and numerous scalps of the enemy attested the triumph of the conquering party.

The Indian wigwams are now replaced by a well-built fort, where the soldiers cultivate a farm for supplying the garrison with food. The whistle of the steamboat as she passes from Mendota to the Fort, is heard instead of the cry of the painted warrior. The fort has a half-crown battery fronting the river, and the top of the bastions commands an extensive and imposing prospect. Towards the West a noble plateau is spread out, with a gently undulating surface, which is diversified with numerous miniature groves, while the intervening prairie is watered with frequent lakes of striking loveliness. As we follow the valley of the Mississippi, the landscape assumes a sterner and bolder appearance; the hills rise abruptly from the shore; a dense mist indicates the locality of the falls; while in the distance, towards the East, the white houses of St. Paul glitter in the sun-light.

A more pleasing view is presented, as we look up the valley of the St. Peter's. The river winds gracefully between its green banks, which gradually slope upwards from the water's edge, and form a succession of natural terraces. These afford an attractive prospect of serene repose and exquisite beauty. A mountain called "Pilate Knob," 262 feet above the level of the Mississippi, is seen at the distance of two miles from Fort Snelling, up the river, from the summit of which, we may look at a wide extent of beautiful country, spreading out in every direction in a charming panorama.

The new city of St. Peter's, or as it is called by the Indians, Mendota, is situated opposite Fort Snelling. The river at this point has a width of 100 yards, and at all stages of the water, admits the passage of steamboats to Little Rapids, a distance of forty-five miles. The banks of the St. Peter's and its tributaries, for a great extent, are distinguished not only for their romantic beauty of scenery, but for their admirable agricultural capacities, rivalling, in this respect, the most fertile regions of the north-west.

BROWN'S CASCADE.

On the small streams which flow into the Mississippi from the West, are several water-falls and rapids, deserving the attention of the admirers of natural scenery. The one represented in the engraving, is known by the name of Brown's Cascade. This charming water-fall is on the road from Fort Snelling to the Falls of St. Anthony. Essentially unlike that cataract, it is remarkable for its soft and delicate beauty, almost reminding the spectator of a creation of artistic fancy. It has no sublime nor awful features, but combines a rare union of qualities to delight the cultivated taste. A small but lovely stream of water, five yards wide, with a gentle current, winds through the undulating prairies, until it reaches the verge of a precipice, over which it falls into a basin below, the distance of 45 feet. It meets with no obstruction, but descends in a regular curve, until it strikes the pool, where it emerges from the white foam produced on the surface, and glides along its downward course. This cascade emits a volume of spray, which in the shining sun produces a beautiful Iris. The effect of the spray upon the surrounding vegetation is distinctly marked. In its vicinity the plants have a more luxuriant growth, and their leaves are colored with a more vivid green than elsewhere. An arch has been excavated behind this cascade by the action of the spray.

DRAWN AFTER NATURE

For the Proprietor: HERRMANN J. MEYER.

BROWN'S FALL

(MINNESOTA)

Published for HERRMANN J. MEYER. 164. William Street. NEWYORK.

DRAWN AFTER NATURE

For the Proprietor: HERRMANN J. MEYER.

WHEELING in VIRGINIA

Published for HERRMANN J. MEYER. 15½ William-Str. NEW-YORK.

WHEELING.

ONE year after the Declaration of Independence, Wheeling was a scattered village of twenty-five log huts. The dwellers upon the Atlantic coast thought of it as the uttermost boundary desirable for civilized life; and told over and over again at their firesides, the story of Daniel Boone, who had left even Wheeling far behind. During the whole time of the revolution, it was a menaced frontier settlement, in the "dark and bloody ground." The waters of the Ohio rippled before its narrow settlement, oftentimes red with the gore of Indian and white man. The cold-blooded Governor Dunmore sent to it repeatedly his Indian allies, to murder and to ravage. And hard by the new site of the Suspension Bridge, had been erected a fort, which christened with the name of Fincastle, was better known through the revolution as Fort Henry. So proud were the claims of the impassioned orator of Virginia, that his fame was invoked by a frontier garrison, who gave their place of refuge his name.

The revolution ceased—westward rolled the tide of emigration—the log huts of Wheeling became cabins, and from cabins passed away into the shape of compact dwellings and stores. The old Dominion began to be proud of her thriving town, which bade fair to become the Queen City of the West. At one time the hopes of Virginia were fairly budded in this respect, but afterwards decayed under the increase of Pittsburgh upon the north, and Cincinnatti to the southward. So that Wheeling may now be treated of as a city, which cannot fail to increase in size and importance, (because it is American,) but which will always be comparatively insignificant, compared with more prosperous neighbors.

At the time of the census of 1840, its white males were 3,836 in number, and its white females, 3,676. Its colored males were 128, and female colored persons, 138. The slaves were 107 in number, with a double preponderance of females. Which made the population of the city, 7885. Ten years afterwards, the Marshal of the Census, in his rounds about western Virginia, found that the population wanted three thousand of a doubling since his predecessor was busied with the same errand. He returned the white males at 6,564; the white females at 6,407; the colored males at 97; the colored females at 110; while the contiguity of free soil and the machinery of the underground railroad, had diminished the desirableness to masters of purchased labor, and thinned the number of slaves to forty-four. This was an increase very fair to calculate, but not such an one which its oldest inhabitants desired. They thought of the coal fields about, and the plantations behind, and the farms before, across the Ohio river—calculating with enthusiasm the facilities for an extended domestic commerce. But they became painfully aware how disadvantageous were shallow channels for a magnificent river, and how powerful was neighboring competition.

The great national road, (now an enterprise of the past, which becomes Lilliputian in its proportions of projection, stretched by the side of the Western railroad, which is destined before many years, to urge its iron sinews into the surf of the Pacific Ocean,) made of Wheeling a way station—connected as were the ends of the road at the river's bank by the great Suspension Bridge. Scarcely an emigrant or a traveller of business or pleasure, but passed through Wheeling. Its avenues, ten years ago, were thronged with stages, (which had descended or were about to ascend, the Alleghanies,) as is Broadway with its roaring omnibusses to-day. Now the citizen sadly misses them, and standing in the broad avenue of the Cumberland road, might say with Buchanan Read,

"But I miss the crowded coaches,
And the drivers' bugle horn—
Miss the crowd of jovial teamsters
Filling buckets at the wells,
With their trains from Conestoga,
And their orchestras of bells."

For the driver's bugle horn has given way to the engineers shrill whistle, and scores of sooty brakemen attached to the Baltimore and Ohio Railroad, are but sorry substitutes for the jovial teamsters. Truly might this same citizen of Wheeling continue with our poet,—

"Ancient highway thou art vanquished;
The usurper of the vale
Rolls in fiery iron rattle,
Exultations on the gale."

Placed by its railroad beyond the care of low water and neighboring competition, Wheeling may soon assume a greater importance.

Its situation is amid the romantic scenery of the Ohio; and the visitor who may stray among the deserted adjacent coal pits, or who may be wearied with the dirty atmosphere of the place which defines the supremacy of the factory and the workshop, has but to ascend a most beautiful hill in the rear of the city, and gaze upon the landscape about and beyond. Below him the Ohio's current, (still somewhat sooty from contact with the wharves of Pittsburg, ninety-five miles above,) slips noiselessly down to salute Cincinnatti and Louisville, and finally find its purity absorbed in the turbid embrace of the Mississippi. The city is full of bustle and energy. One wide and principal street filled with stores, opens before the view, while intersecting it are cross streets, rich with shops and studded with beautiful dwellings. There too is the Suspension Bridge. As we survey it in the picture, we are loth to believe so beautiful and useful a structure (after an Ex-Chancellor of the Empire State had taken all testimony *pro* and *con* upon the subject,) had been solemnly adjudged a nuisance, by the highest law court in the land. And so adjudged from the clamors of the steamboat interest, been altered in height to permit the passage of the highest smoke-pipes known to Ohio waters. At the levee of the water front, lie numerous steamboats, which ascend to Pittsburg or descend to Louisville, as trade may govern. There is even a sloop near by, which is brave enough to think of a voyage to the waters of the Mexican Gulf, there to become a coaster—a sloop builded from wood that grew a thousand miles away from the ocean.

Such would be a fair view of the city whose picture our readers now gaze upon. Its infancy was eminently romantic, but its maturity pays a most valuable tribute to the genius of practical life. Not many years ago a western frontier town, its oldest inhabitant is to-day as it were, a citizen of the Atlantic seaboard; for in one day he may rattle through the Alleghanies in the rail-car to the city of Baltimore, and pay what homage he pleases to the destiny of Atlantic Commerce, in which his birth-place may soon become a more extended participant.

THE CLIFFS BELOW ST. PAUL.

THE banks of the river below St. Paul, rise into almost perpendicular bluffs, covered with abrupt and craggy rocks, in the crevices of which, eagles and other wild birds build their nests. A few dwarf cedars find a scanty nourishment in the vegetable mould which is gathered in these crevices, stretching their roots by a curious instinct, in every quarter, in search of food.

At various points of the Upper Mississippi, we find bluffs of a similar character, with fine rolling prairie land in the rear, composing a region of the richest agricultural resources. Groves of timber are seen at intervals, filled with various species of oak, hickory, maple, elm, and so forth. The pine forests which abound on the St. Croix, present an agreeable variety, while the low ground of the swamps furnishes a luxuriant growth of tamarask, or black larch. The eye of the traveller is often attracted by the rafts of pine lumber, which pass down the river from the mills at the Falls, where vast quantities of boards and shingles are manufactured, from the forests on the river banks. On all the streams, saw-mills have been erected, which do a large amount of business. During the winter months, the woods resound with the axe of the lumberman, the crash of falling trees, and the shouts of the laborer. The logs are drawn by ox teams to the water's edge, and are floated down to the mills on return of spring. After reaching the Great River, several of the smaller rafts are joined in one, and in this form, floating down the current, and guided by the long oars of the steersman, are taken to market. A little hut is erected on the raft for the protection of the crew, who are divided into two sets or watches, one of which is on duty both night and day, the danger of the current requiring constant vigilance. The towns and cities, which are rapidly springing up along the river, are furnished in part by these rafts, with their

DRAWN AFTER NATURE.

For the Proprietor: HERRMANN J. MEYER.

BLUFFS BELOW ST PAUL

(MISSISSIPPI-RIVER)

Published for HERRMANN J. MEYER. 164 William-Street NEWYORK.

DRAWN AFTER NATURE

For the Proprietor HERRMANN J. MEYER.

MOUTH OF THE S^T CROIX RIVER

(MINNESOTA)

Published for HERRMANN J. MEYER, 164. William Str. NEWYORK.

supplies of lumber. St. Louis opens a central market, and many of the rafts are broken up at that city.

The pine forests of Michigan, Wisconsin, and Minnesota, constitute an important source of the wealth of the region bordering on the north-eastern tributaries of the Mississippi. They give employment to a large number of emigrants from the eastern States, who, though rough in exterior, and often regarded by strangers as persons of a desperate character, are in fact not surpassed by any class of citizens for intelligence, good morals, and kindness of feeling. Often the sons of wealthy families adopt the lumbering business as a temporary pursuit, until they can obtain the means to purchase land, or engage in some more permanent occupation.

Near the scene presented in the engraving, is the Indian village of Le Petit Corbeau, (the Little Crow.) In 1849, this consisted of about 40 lodges, and 300 souls, of the Kapasia band of the Dahcotahs. On the high bluffs in the rear of the village, several scaffolds were erected, on which were placed the bodies of deceased warriors, enclosed in rude coffins, or swathed in blankets, while flags, which floated from elevated staffs, indicated the ceremonies of Indian sepulture. The Dacotahs, as well as several other tribes, make this temporary disposition of the remains of the dead. After a few months of exposure, the bodies are removed from the scaffold, and buried in the ground. According to a Dahcotah superstition, the Indian needs the pressure of the earth on his breast, after recent decease, and desires to be placed in an elevated position, in order that he may still behold the scenes and transactions in which he took part during life.

A large boulder on the opposite bank, near Little Crow village, is an object of religious veneration among the Indians. It is called Red Rock, from the pigment with which it is colored. The offerings which are brought to it, consisting of eagle feathers, branches of the willow, and esculent roots, are painted with vermilion.

The narrowest part of the river below the Falls of St. Anthony, is near this place. Here the river contracts to the width of 120 yards, passing through an undulating prairie country, of remarkable loveliness. The banks are of moderate height, and no islands obstruct the free passage of the water. The ground slope on either side, is dotted by frequent farm houses, partly concealed by leafy groves. There is a settlement of French Canadians, of about thirty families in this vicinity, who cultivate the fertile meadows for some distance along the river. A few miles further down is the Mouth of the St. Croix.

The embouchure of the St. Croix, presents a scene of exquisite romantic beauty. On each side, luxuriant groves of forest trees throw their shadows over the transparent surface of the water, which serves as a mirror to reflect the fresh green of the foliage, while in the back ground, the whole region spreads forth in the wild fertility of nature.

At the junction of the two rivers a small village, called Point Douglass, stands on a sloping prairie, presenting a charming view of the river, and in itself, forming a picturesque object in the distance. Opposite the mouth of the St. Croix, the bank of the Mississippi is low and rocky, affording an eligible site for a town, with a safe and excellent landing. The entrance of the St. Croix is by a narrow channel of not over 100 yards in width, but soon after the river expands into the dimensions of a lake, three-quarters of a mile wide, and surrounded by a delicious landscape. The water is pure and limpid, and contains a great variety of fish.

The banks of the river present no abrupt and lofty bluffs, but descend by a gentle slope to the water's edge. The adjacent prairie is covered at intervals with smiling farm-houses, which speak well for the fertility of the soil, and the thrift of the settler. The lake is navigable for steamboats to the town of Stillwater, where a brisk lumber trade gives considerable animation to the place. At a greater distance up the St. Croix, it abounds with rapids, and affords the tourist some of the wildest and most striking scenery in the valley of the Upper Mississippi.

DRAWN AFTER NATURE. For the Proprietor: HERRMANN J. MEYER.

NAUVOO

(MISSISSIPPI)

Published for HERRMANN J. MEYER. 164. William-Str. NEWYORK.

NAUVOO.

NAUVOO—"The City of Beauty!" This is surely no misnomer, if we regard only locality; for very few sites for a city are there on the banks of the great river, from its source to its mouth, more lovely or more desirable, than that of persecuted Nauvoo—the Mormon city, now no more.

From the eastern bank of the Mississippi, in the county of Hancock, State of Illinois, nearly two hundred miles above St. Louis, about a dozen miles above the foot of the Lower Rapids and the mouth of the Des Moines, and one hundred and twenty from the capital of the State, slopes gently into the stream a semi-alluvial point of land, sufficiently spacious for a populous city; while on the opposite bank, in the State of Iowa, rises the pleasant hamlet of Montrose. Such is the site of departed Nauvoo. Some twenty or thirty years ago, when this land first came into market, it was entered at the government price by a Connecticut Yankee; but it seems never to have realized the sanguine anticipations which the loveliness of its site had inspired; and, indeed, the very existence of the spot seems to have been quite unknown, save to voyagers on the Upper Mississippi, until it arrested the eye of the Mormon Prophet, and was destined to a world-wide notoriety as the Medina, if not the Mecca of the Mormon faith. This renown was consequent on the Hegira, or rather on the Exodus of the Saints of the Latter Days, from Missouri in the mid winter of 1838, the second expulsion to which this deluded and unfortunate sect had been subjected. Of its origin, and rise, and growth, and history, every one knows. Whether the name of Joseph Smith is destined to retain the immortality of a Mahomet—of the Mahomet of the nineteenth century—remains for coming time to tell; but it is very certain that the faith of which he was founder, sealed by his blood as its first martyr, has found more proselytes within the first climacteric of its existence, and that too without the enforcement of the sword, and beyond the limits of the continent of its birth, than did that of the imposter of Mecca, with all its carnal auxilliaries to aid its progress. Every one knows the birth-place of the American Mahomet, hardly less than that of the Mahomet of Arabia; and the little inland town of Palmyra, in the State of New York, bids fair to become hardly less noted the world over for the nativity of one prophet, than is the famed city of Mecca for that of the other; although whether it will ever become the recipient of shrines and the gathering spot of pilgrims, futurity alone can determine.

How Joseph Smith was one of several children of humble parents, born early in the present century—how he, as a boy, albeit by no means a good boy, or an intelligent boy, was favored with visions, and dreams, and revelations from the unseen world—how, at the age of eighteen years, in the month of September, 1823, it was announced to him by an angel, that, as the apostle and prophet of a purified faith, the records of the lost tribes of Israel, the aboriginal nations of America, were to be revealed to him graven on golden plates, buried on the summit of the Hill of Cumorah—how, four years later, in the month of September, 1827, the golden plates were in fact finally given him—how, meanwhile, he led a nomadic life, seeking after hidden treasures, and at length secured one in a young girl of New Harmony, whom he carried off and married—how, nearly at the same time, he secured another treasure in a manuscript novel, written by a pious clergyman of New Salem, in the State of Ohio, a dozen years before, purporting to have been transcribed from records buried in the earth by Moroni, son of Mormon—how that he then professed to commence the translation of the golden plates, which none but he ever saw, and how an honest farmer, with more acres than brains, was reduced to beggary by contributions for the publication of the Book of Mormon, which proved to be only the religious fiction of the village pastor, vilely interpolated—how, from only half a dozen disciples, including the prophet's father, two brothers and the victimized farmer, in the summer of 1830, a Church of Jesus Christ of Latter Day Saints, numbering five times as many persons, was formed at Manchester in New York, and how persecution at once began, and within a year, had swelled the number to a thousand converts—how Cowdrey, Vigdon and Pratt, became proselytes, and Kirtland, Ohio, became a rendezvous for the faithful, and a bank was established and broke, and Smith and Vigdon were tarred and feathered, and how, warned by special revelation, the whole host shortly after moved off to the western frontier to Mount Zion, the ancient Eden, near the town of Independence, in Jackson county, Missouri—how the saints had now increased in number to thousands, and their apostles to hundreds, and how persecution again arose, and many fled into an adjoining county, and many sought refuge at Kirtland—how, during four years, from 1834 to 1838, only maltreatment and misfortune were experienced, until at length expelled from Ohio and Missouri, the whole vast host sought refuge on the banks of the Mississippi, in Illinois; is not all this written in books, and is it not known as the concurrent history of the present generation, by all who have read, or who have heard read the journals of the day? Yet, all this pertains to the primitive history of Nauvoo; for from all this did Nauvoo derive its origin.

The houses at first constructed were of wood, and many of them of logs, not less than a thousand being erected within three years; while, in imitation of the old French villages, each was surrounded by its own yard and garden. The population rapidly increased, until it reached some 15,000 or 20,000 souls, large numbers of the new proselytes being the fruit of the preaching of Mormon missionaries among the poorer classes, the small farmers, and the operatives of the manufacturing towns of Great Britain, who, oppressed at home, were probably quite as much converts to the new land of promise, as to the new faith. Of this thriving capital, Smith was prophet, priest and king—the mayor and the autocrat. He was, also, the chief publican, the chief store-keeper of the place; and pleasantly varied his labors in preaching and baptizing, by dealing out sugar by the pound and whiskey by the glass. He was, also, generalissimo of all the army and navy of Mormonism, and very frequently reviewed the "Nauvoo Legion," surrounded by his staff of pretty girls in black velvet hats and habits, on spirited steeds, upon the broad plains of the vicinage. Occasionally, too, he started out on a missionary excursion, and preached, not altogether without effect, to the Iowa savages on the frontier. A temple was commenced likewise, on the most elevated spot in the place, and on a peculiar plan specially revealed to the prophet. With pomp and pageant, and strange ceremonial, the first stone was laid on the 6th day of April, 1841, and the edifice was five years in course of construction. Its material was a white and compact limestone, quarried near the city; its architect was a "Gentile" named Weeks; its order was a composite of Grecian, Roman and Egyptian, to which the word Mormon can alone do justice; its dimensions were one hundred and twenty-eight feet long, by eighty-eight wide, with walls sixty-five feet high, and a cupola one hundred and sixty-three feet above the ground. It was entered by three Roman portals, and lighted by numerous windows in the same style, between all of which were pilasters, ornamented at the base with an inverted crescent, and at the capital with a human head, sustained by two hands grasping a trumpet! It was two stories high with a basement, an attic, and an intermediate half-story between the first and the second. In the basement stood the Baptismal font, supported by twelve huge and solemn-looking oxen, of white limestone, with horns of fearful length; while around were twelve preparation rooms, and two others, smaller ones, for recording clerks. Ascending to the first floor by means of a double flight of stone stairs, you entered the great hall for worship, into which was poured a perfect flood of light from sixteen large windows, eight on either side. There was a gallery for the choir, and three pulpits for the preachers, over which was read the inscription, "The Lord has beheld our sacrifice: come after us." The second floor was in all respects like the first, and between the two ran two long narrow rooms for the elders, the entire depth of the edifice, lighted by eight circular windows each. The attic was made up of one large room and twelve small ones, also lighted by circular windows, and the doors secured by heavy locks, the design of which seems to have been never revealed. The edifice was calculated to seat three thousand persons. Two flights of stairs meeting at the base of the tower, conducted from the floor in the front portico of the edifice to the roof, which was designed as a public promenade for the town. The view from this spot was extensive and beautiful, while that from the lofty summit above was, if possible, yet more so—a limitless expanse of prairie, extending to the horizon on one side, and an equally limitless expanse of forest, rolling away towards the setting sun on the other, while the bright Mississippi glided like a thread of silver through its enamelled banks, and among its emerald islands, and went joyously sparkling over its rapids between.

The edifice was of massive construction—the stone walls being some six feet thick; and it seemed rather a fortress than a temple—a place of refuge rather than of worship. It was, doubtless, designed with an equal view to each. Every stone was laid by a Mormon; every person employed on it was a disciple of the faith save the architect; each man devoted a little of his time and of his substance to its construction; and it is estimated to have cost, at a fair valuation of labor and material, on its completion, nearly a million of dollars! It is certain that it was offered for sale in 1846 by the departing Mormons when completed, for $200,000; and equally certain that it brought but the fourth part of that sum when purchased in 1848.

The tales with reference to this edifice have been ridiculous in their exaggeration. That it was an imposing structure is most true; but that it was "the most magnificent edifice in this land or any other," is simply preposterous. It was, in fact, rather grotesque in its style than grand; and one hardly knew whether to laugh or to be solemn at its unique decorations. There have been similar exaggerations as touching the population and importance of the town itself. That its population rapidly increased is unquestionable, but at its maximum, it never exceeded twenty thousand souls; and, among many sedate and industrious people, there were, also, many worthless vagabonds, the outcasts and offscourings of all other communities in the world. Public, or even private enterprise among them, seemed quite unknown; and the only exhibition of religious enterprise, was beheld in the construction of the massive fortalice which they called a temple. Other public edifices there were none; and the private residences were of the very plainest if not of the very meanest character. The municipal economy, policy and regulations, were altogether inefficient. Broad and unpaved country roads running at right angles, were dignified with the generic appellation of streets, though often unhonored with specific names. Manufacturing, mercantile, commercial and artistic industry, seemed utterly unknown. The whole population, so far as it was devoted to anything, seemed devoted to agriculture. The daily, almost hourly steamers, navigating the upper Mississippi, passing the town, rarely stopped, save perchance to land a company of foreign immigrants, or of curious tourists; and the Landing, if such that might be termed, which Landing was none, presented a very different aspect from the Landings at all other places on the river.

Indeed, Nauvoo was a complete anomaly among Western towns. Its rambling streets—its singular structures, each isolated in its individual garden-spot—its broadcast aspect, sprinkled as were its houses over the vast slope—its silent and abandoned appearance, though it was thronged with population—the entire absence of enterprise, and the bustle of business and din of industry—the sluggish, desperate, downcast looks of the men, and the care-worn, languid, shame-faced countenances of the women, while even the children seemed not to indulge in the noisy sports which befit their age—these features and characteristics distinguished Nauvoo, first and last, from every other place. In population, such as it was, it increased more rapidly than its neighbors, and from very obvious causes; but in commercial, mercantile, manufacturing improvement, or even in agricultural importance, it could bear no comparison with the thriving towns all around it, with Hannibal, Quincy, Warsaw, Burlington, Bloomington, Davenport, Galena, to say nothing of those of the interior, more distant from navigable streams.

And, as was the City of the Saints in the autumn of 1840, when first visited by the writer, at its very commencement, and as it was when again visited in the summer of 1844, at the very zenith of its prime, such, doubtless, would it always have continued. There were in the very elements of its existence and its society inherent vices, which must inevitably have checked enterprise and advancement in all those things, which, in the view of the age and the country, go to make up importance. It more resembled a sleepy old town in the heart of Germany or Italy, than one on the banks of the great artery of young and wide-awake America. It had no "spur to the sides of its intent"—no main-spring—no impelling-force—nothing to kindle and foster emulation and enterprise, while there was much to smother and to stifle both. It had all the drawbacks of the Quaker, the Shaker, or the Moravian communities, without their industry, their propriety, their unimpeachable morality. Cut off by selfish policy from all interest in or connexion with the whole world beside, its people cared no more for all the rest of the State of Illinois, of which it was a portion, than did all the rest of the State of Illinois care for them. Like the Miller of Mansfield—

> "They cared for nobody, no, not they,
> For nobody cared for them."

Nobody, save, indeed, the candidate for office, who sought their thousand or two of votes, always thrown in a mass as dictated by the prophet. And these votes alone it was which gave them political importance. Emasculated by vicious habits—false morality—false religion—a false system of society and a false condition of things altogether—

the place rather vegetated than grew—remained stationary rather than flourished; while by the people of the neighboring villages the inhabitants were viewed with an odium, distrust, antipathy and contempt, which the Mormons failed not with usury to reciprocate.

As for the system of religious faith, though based on the Bible, and professing the cardinal doctrines of Christianity, upon it had been grafted most fatal and pernicious errors, and most abominable vices. How could it be otherwise with a man like Joe Smith as its high-priest, and an imposture like the "Book of Mormon" for its Bible? What wonder that a degrading polygamy, under the name of "Spiritual wedlock," followed hard on implicit reliance upon "special revelations" to a licentious prophet? That a man like Joseph Smith, ignorant, shallow, feeble-minded, whose only talents were those of the pickpocket, the mountebank and the swindler—mere shrewdness and craft,—should ever, in the middle of a century which we are wont to imagine the most enlightened our world has yet known, and in the middle of a land equally exalted in our estimate, have been able to originate and carry so successfully on such a stupendous and silly fraud as Mormonism, seems utterly incredible. It is, moreover, unspeakably humiliating. Let us refer no more to the impostures of earlier periods, and of other peoples and other lands. What were the Crusades, with their dazzling splendors, pouring Europe on Asia—what the flaming fanaticism and the sweeping proselytism and the fiery falchion of the false prophet, in an age of darkness, and among an almost pagan people, to this?

It was in the month of June, 1844, as already intimated, and during the unparalleled flood of that season, that the writer last visited Nauvoo. Half the country was under water; but the City of the Saints was high and dry—was founded in this regard, at least, "on a rock." But this was its sole superiority. The place was now at the zenith of its power, population, prosperity, importance, if, indeed, it can be said ever to have possessed either of these recommendations. Yet its characteristic features were altogether such as have been outlined. In a long interview with the prophet, at his own house, a plain two-story structure of wood, at once tavern and grocery, was gathered the opinion of him already expressed. Low and shallow cunning alone seemed written on his sensual, silly, unintellectual face. A retreating forehead, prominent nose, small and irresolute eyes, unmeaning lips, bad teeth, and but few of them, an obese and ungainly figure, an almost feminine voice and a nervous timidity of manner—such were the more observable personal traits of the prophet as now recalled. Upon the walls of his bar-room hung a full length portrait of himself, as commander-in-chief of the military force of Nauvoo, in full regimentals; and a full representation likewise of the temple as completed, though then hardly ready for its roof. In an adjoining room, an Egyptian mummy, together with divers metallic plates covered with hieroglyphics, and connected by a ring, were exhibited by the prophet's mother, a very aged and infirm woman, who, poor old soul, with implicit faith, demonstrated their connexion with the revelations of her shameless son—at the charge of a quarter of a dollar a head. Here, also, were two young and handsome, and loosely clad females, a portion, probably, of that spiritual household which the prophet's wife, Emma, had permitted him to introduce under her roof.

Internal discord had for some time, at this period, been raging at Nauvoo. External pressure being removed, internecine strife had begun. Long before this, Cowdrey, Rigdon and others of the prophet's early disciples and fellow impostors had been denounced by him. To them, too, had come "special revelations," and these revelations at times conflicted with those of their spiritual head. Revelation, for example, at times designated fair women as their "spiritual wives," who had already been designated, or who were about to be designated, as favored ones for the prophet's own spiritual seraglio! There were many other causes of variance. At length a newspaper was started by Rigdon and others, in the very city of Nauvoo itself, exposing and denouncing the prophet's abominable vices. This was bearding "the lion in his den, the Douglass in his hall." By his order the press was broken up, and the conductors driven ignominiously from the place. On the very day before the interview alluded to, there had been an *emeute*, and the prophet still wore a bandage on his hand, because of an injury sustained in wrenching a loaded pistol levelled at his head, from the grasp of a foe. The malcontents fled to Carthage, the county town, and with warrants for the arrest of Joseph and Hiram Smith, and of sixteen others who had demolished their press, returned with officers to Nauvoo. But no arrests were made. The law was resisted, and its ministers were driven off. The "power of the county" was ordered out to sustain the government, and the Nauvoo Legion was ordered out to uphold its prophet. Ford, the Governor of Illinois, now personally appeared; and, on his promise of protection and justice, Joseph and Hiram Smith surrendered themselves, and were conducted to Carthage jail. But it was too late now to resist the tornado of popular fury. On the evening of the 27th of June, less than a fortnight after the interview of the writer with the prophet at Nauvoo, a band of armed men, disguised as negroes, rushed on the guard of the jail, drove them from their charge on peril of their lives, and, with repeated rifle-shots, dispatched both victims of their wrath and fled. They were never identified. There was, probably, little effort to identify them.

Thus perished the first martyrs to Mormonism. Its founder was its first victim. His successor was Brigham Young, who still remains the spiritual head of the church. Rigdon and his party fell into disgrace; but they went forth as preachers against the infamous orgies of Nauvoo, and the whole country was roused against the fanatics. Assaults on their settlements, destruction of their property, insults to their persons, incessant infringements with entire impunity on their rights, followed. Their "destiny," was as "manifest" as was that of Israel in Egypt. Another Exodus, the third within nine years, was inevitable; and, in the midwinter of 1846, nearly two thousand Mormons, with their wives and little ones, their flocks and their herds, their oxen and wagons and household stuff, crossed the Mississippi on the ice, and, after a weary way through the wilderness, halted on the Indian frontier of Missouri, beyond Council Bluffs. The residue tarried to complete the temple. This was, at length accomplished, albeit the building of the same, was like unto the building of the temple and the walls of Jerusalem of old, when the builder grasped a trowel in one hand and a sword in the other. Assaults were incessant, and far from bloodless. At length, completed, with barbaric pomp the temple was dedicated; over its portals was inscribed—"Holiness to the Lord," and then the spot was abandoned forever! In the fall of 1848, on the night of October 9th, the edifice fell a sacrifice to the incendiary's torch; and in the spring of 1850, in the month of May, its massive walls were levelled by a hurricane with the soil.

In the autumn of 1846, the last Mormons were expelled by an armed force from the City of Beauty, and henceforth it was to be known by a new name and inhabited by a new people. In 1847, the exiles furnished a battalion for the Mexican war, and marched to Santa Fe. The same summer was commenced the settlement and City of Salt Lake, now the capital of the territory of Utah, established in 1850, of which Young was appointed Governor, and which now has a population of 30,000 souls, half enough to form a State, though the territory is capable of sustaining a million. The strange faith is now diffused over three continents, and is estimated to number converts by the hundreds of thousands—more than one-fourth of which have been furnished by Great Britain!

The career of Brigham Young has been almost as eventful as was that of the Prophet himself. In the year 1830, after divers movings and re-movings, we find him a tanner, in Ontario County, New York, where, having been converted by the "Book of Mormon," three years later he joined the Prophet at Kirtland. In 1838 he migrated with the fraternity to Mount Zion, in Jackson County, Missouri, and thence accompanied them, a year later, to Nauvoo, where he dwelt for seven consecutive years. Driven thence in 1846 to the frontier of Missouri, he suffered his people, of whom he was now the chief, to enlist to the number of five hundred, on requisition of the United States, for the Mexican war. Early the ensuing April he commenced a weary pilgrimage of a thousand miles to the Great Salt Lake, which, with about a hundred and fifty men, he reached late in July. Immediately returning to the frontier for his family, in the spring of 1849 he again went out; and, in 1850, was appointed, by President Fillmore, Governor of the new Territory of Deseret.

For some years after the final abandonment of Nauvoo, in September, 1846, the City of Beauty presented the very picture of desolation. The whole site of the once populous place now bristled with the chimnies of the dismantled houses, which remained as relics, only because they could not be easily removed. "The walls of Balclutha were desolate. The thistle shook there its lonely head; the moss whistled to the wind. The fox looked out from the windows; the rank grass of the wall waved round his head." Shattered casements, broken-down doors, overthrown enclosures, unweeded garden-plats, deserted streets, were the sad records of a persecuted race—the sure traces of sin, and sorrow, and suffering, and shame. But the fortress-temple still towered grandly over all, with its lofty spire, on its commanding site, a monument of fanaticism, imposture and blind belief.

But all this has passed away, and the City of Beauty of the Mormons is now the City of Equality of the Socialist. Nauvoo is now Icaria. Three years ago the celebrated Cabet, whose name appears amid events of the French Revolution of 1848, came to the United States, followed or preceded by some two or three hundred men, women and children, mostly of the laboring class, composing his community of Icarians. In his *exposé* of causes for this immigration *en masse*, he assigns as chief a league between the government, the aristocracy and the clergy to persecute his people and himself. To emigrate to America and found a new Icaria in the wilderness was, therefore, resolved on; and the recent expulsion of another peculiar people presented a somewhat perilous refuge at Nauvoo. To civilize the desert, to create a State based on community of interests, to erect an asylum for the exiles of Europe, these are proclaimed the objects of the new Icaria; while "All for Each, and Each for All" is its motto. The land has been leased only, a tract of some five thousand acres in the State of Iowa having been purchased for a permanent home. Their principal structure is a large one of wood, two stories high and very long, in which many are lodged and all are fed. The men are said to number nearly two hundred, the women about seventy, and the children forty or fifty, and all are, apparently, happy and content, especially the two latter classes. Their diet is exceedingly simple, consisting chiefly of soup and bread, which is partaken of twice a day by the whole community, summoned by a trumpet to the long pine tables on which the simple repast is spread. A press has been established, from which issue two weekly papers, one in the German language and one in the English, but none in the French; a large school-house has been constructed of ruins of the Mormon temple; a brewery, a distillery, a saw-mill, a grist-mill, a library, a theatre, a cabinet of physic and chemistry, and a small arsenal of hunting guns have been established, and some twenty acres of land have been put in cultivation for vegetables. Game is plentiful, and so are fish; and boats and nets have been constructed for the capture of the latter.

Icarianism is declared to be a mixture of individualism and communism. The lodgings are individual—each man lodging with his wife and family; but the boarding is common, and so is all the property; and each is fed, lodged and clothed from the common fund, according to his necessities. All religious opinions are tolerated, fraternity and justice being deemed the sole essentials of Christianity, and happiness in a future state the destiny of all. Men and women labor alike in the workshop or in the field. The recreations are lectures, concerts, readings, dramatic performances and the like. Women enjoy the same social rights as men, and have a voice in the general council, but no vote. Marriage is promoted, and the contract is declared inviolable, though, when proving insupportable, may be dissolved. Equality in education, as in food and everything else, is declared the right of all. The community provides for the helpless, old or young, and for the ill; health is secured rather by diet and mode of life than by medicine; and the physician is a public officer, responsible for the health of the community!

The President of Icaria, Cabet, to whom the world is indebted for this declaration of principles and purposes, is said to be a sincere, shrewd man, with more benevolence of heart than force of mind, greatly respected by his flock, among whom reign harmony and content. To enter the community application, examination, a probation of four months, a two-thirds vote of the Assembly, and a contribution of property, amounting to, at least, eighty dollars, to the general fund are required. To leave the community it is only necessary to give notice, and to receive one-half or four-fifths of the original contribution, according as the person was definitively or provisionally received, together with his bed, his wardrobe, and his utensils of labor. Expulsion, upon a vote of the Assembly, is the penalty prescribed for violation of the laws of the community; and the candidate for admission "must be temperate—must have no necessity for tobacco or strong drinks—must be decent in words and acts, must be industrious and prudent —must believe in Christianity—must be married, or must engage to become so."

The population of Nauvoo, at the present time, is said to be some three thousand persons. The widow of the Prophet Smith, with her son, a young man of twenty, yet resides there, both being decidedly opposed to Mormonism, and the former having again become a wife. Below the town, some thousands of Mormons were encamped early the past summer, preparatory to migration to the City of Salt Lake. The site of the Temple is held by the Icarians, the western front of the structure looking down on the river and visible for miles around, alone remaining to mark the spot. The Methodists have here a church, and the Catholics a parish.

DRAWN AFTER NATURE

For the Proprietor: HERRMANN J. MEYER.

NEW HARMONY

Published for HERRMANN J. MEYER. 164. William-Str. NEWYORK.

NEW HARMONY.

THERE are few places in the West, which, for attractiveness of locality or eventfulness of history, offer so much of interest as the scene of the far-famed social experiments of George Rapp and Robert Owen, on the eastern bank of the Wabash, about seventy miles from its mouth, and sixty from Vincennes, the nearest point on the Ohio, Mount Vernon, being fifteen miles distant. The village stands on a high plain which was once the bottom of the river, and is girdled by a crescent of beautiful hills several miles in extent, affording pasturage for numberless sheep. The Wabash, which is here the dividing line between Indiana and Illinois, is navigable at all seasons for keel boats of forty tons to the mouth of the White River, some miles below Palmyra in the latter State. An alluvial island of some three thousand acres stretches along the stream, separated by a slough or cut-off two miles in extent from the main land. A belt of forest separates the town from the low meadows along the stream, liable to inundation, and devoted to pasturage. The scenery around, diversified by hill and vale, grove, garden, orchard and cultivated fields, is most charming. The soil of the bottom-lands is a rich alluvion of sand and loam with a super-stratum of deep vegetable mould. The locality is high and healthy. The geological basis is a heavy brown free stone, easily quarried for building. Coal and timber abound. The river supplies abundance of fish, and the forests abundance of game; while a vast water-power for manufactures is afforded by the bayou or cut-off, which separates the island from the main land.

Yet, with all these advantages, New Harmony never has been, and probably never will be any thing more than a very beautiful, and very unique little town. It was first settled in 1814, by the followers of George Rapp, under the name of Harmonists. This religious sect owed its origin to a schism in the Lutheran Church, in

Wirtemberg, Germany, and seems to have formed a Society intermediate between the Shakers and the United Brethren. The association appears not at all to have contemplated the advantages of co-operative industry, but to have been founded on religious conviction, and to have had as its motto that verse in the fourth chapter of the Acts of the Apostles, which declares the primitive Christians to have had "all things in common." Their rules were severe; and, in order, neatness, industry and subordination, they rivalled the Shakers, while their system of government was as completely theocratical as that of the Plymouth Pilgrims. Like those Pilgrims, also, of an earlier day, they left the old world for the new, for the sake of a larger liberty, religious and civil, and in 1804, led by Rapp, their pastor and chief, their spiritual and temporal head, a hundred and fifty families crossed the ocean, and in the autumn of that year commenced a settlement in Butler County, on Beaver River, in the State of Pennsylvania, which they called Harmony. Here, for years, amid a howling wilderness, they suffered and struggled, enduring toil, hardship, penury and disease. Discouraged, worn out, many left the community, but prosperity at length smiled on the remnant that remained, and "the wilderness blossomed as the rose," and the hamlet of Harmony became the "sweet Auburn" of all that region.

Comparative opulence having now been achieved, a more favorable location was desired, and, in 1813, young Frederick Rapp, adopted son of their founder, was sent forth on the mission. Having traversed six of the Western States in the search, he at length fixed on a spot which embraced the four requisites prescribed—health, fertility, water-power and water-communication; and, in the spring and summer of 1814, having disposed of their village for $100,000, the adventurous Germans to the number of eight hundred repaired to the chosen site and named it *New* Harmony, in memory of the old. But the wilderness was again around them; disease and death were again among them; toil and privation, hardship and destitution were again their lot. But they still triumphed over all obstacles, and, in the fall of 1824, only ten years later, their thirty thousand acres of land with its improvements, stock and buildings were valued at one million of dollars. This has been cited as "an instance of accumulation in the laborious professions to which history affords no parallel." In 1804, the property of the entire community on the bleak banks of the Beaver was not worth intrinsically the sum of $25, while in 1825, on the banks of the smiling Wabash, each man, woman and child was entitled, on a fair division of profits, to $2500!

The town was laid off with most Quaker-like regularity into squares, being cut at right angles by four streets running north and south, and six others running east and west, and presenting in this regard, as in most other regards, indeed, a striking contrast to the rambling old villages of the French on the banks of the Mississippi. The closely-enclosed and highly-cultivated farms and neat meadows of the former, presented a contrast equally striking to the vast common fields and unimproved "commons" of the latter. More than a hundred structures, brick, frame and log, were erected, some of which were spacious and almost splendid. The Town Hall, for example, the public house for all religious or civic assemblages was constructed of brick in the form of a Greek cross, one hundred and twenty-five feet in length. The lower floor was occupied by one large room, entered by a door at the centre of each wing, with a lofty ceiling supported by massive pillars; while smaller apartments occupied the wings and floor above. Half a dozen boarding houses of brick, some ninety feet by seventy in dimensions, were, also, constructed in the old Dutch style of architecture, with awkward hipped roofs and dormer windows. They are said, however, to be very commodious, and two of them are now taverns. None of these edifices, indeed, had any equals at the time, either in construction or dimension, in towns of similar size in the West. A public Granary was also erected, and is, to this day, the first object to arrest the traveller's eye as he approaches the place, though it looks more like a fort than any thing else, with its massive walls of brick and stone, its loop-holed walls and its tiled roof. And, indeed, it is said to have been constructed as much with a view to the protection of the Harmonists themselves as of their grain; and more than once afforded the peaceful Germans a refuge from the lawless men who at that early period haunted the country and invaded the frontier villages for plunder. The old structure is now the laboratory and museum of Dr. David Dale Owen.

But the Rappites did not confine themselves to the useful or indispensible in the improvements of their new home. Extensive orchards containing the best varieties of the apple, pear, plum and peach were planted; a botanic garden and a green-house were established; and an extensive vineyard afforded fruit and wine sufficient for the whole community. An ornamental spot called The Labyrinth, was also laid out, composed of intricate and serpentine walks, with groves of bushes and gardens of flowers and shrubs, and a small temple in the centre, rude without but neat within covered with vines,—the whole emblematic of that Harmony so difficult to obtain, so pleasant to enjoy. But pleasant though it was, it seems not to have been sufficiently so to tempt others to enter, nor to prevent the Rappites themselves from looking back with yearning hearts to their old home on the banks of the Beaver, from which ten years of absence had not served to wean them.

At this period, in the fall of 1824, a stranger, of whom they had heard as a philosopher of a new school, and the founder of a new system of Society, came among them. He was a man some fifty years of age, intelligent and sanguine, yet not an enthusiast; and rather a plodding, persevering, practical, business man, than a fanatical reformer. This man was Robert Owen, of New Lanark, Scotland. A native of Montgomeryshire, in the Principality of Wales, at the age of ten he went to London, and finally to Manchester, where for some years he was engaged in constructing machinery and spinning cotton. Thence he repaired to Nêw Lanark, and there for twenty-five years devoted himself to devising remedies for, and preventives to the evils of the social system now pervading Christendom. The new world presenting to him a more open field for the dissemination of his doctrines, he embarked for New York, where he arrived in the month of November, 1824; and having heard of the village of the Rappites on the banks of the Wabash as for sale, and deeming it an excellent spot on which to test his system, at once repaired to New Harmony, purchased the whole settlement for $190,000, and invited "the industrious and well-disposed of all nations" to join him.

As for the Harmonists, they went back to Pennsylvania and settled at the town of Economy on the Ohio, about twenty miles below Pittsburgh. In 1832, some of them were led off by Count Leon, a new prophet, and settled at Phillipsburgh, on the opposite bank of the river half a dozen miles below; but their Zion soon exploded and they went home. In 1847, the venerable Rapp died at Economy, full of years and honors, and was there buried. The place numbers now between one and two thousand inhabitants, noted for industry and sobriety, and the society has several good mills. Among the peculiar views of the Rappites is said to be one respecting marriage—husbands and wives in their community living as such only every seventh year—the year of the Jewish jubilee.

The purchase of Mr. Owen consisted of thirty thousand acres of valuable land, three thousand acres of which had been cultivated by the Harmonists. There were, also, nineteen detached farms comprising nearly six hundred acres of improved land cultivated chiefly by tenants, and several extensive orchards, gardens and vineyards.

People of all lands and languages at once flocked to the new Utopia, and ere long some eight or nine hundred persons, embracing many women and children, had become members. Every State then in the Union save two was represented, and almost every country of Northern Europe. Some needy and idle persons availed themselves of Mr. Owen's liberal offers; but many who repaired to the spot were men of talent, property, standing and worth. Among these were Dr. Gerard Frost, Dr. Price, and Thomas Say the distinguished naturalist, all of Philadelphia. Mr. William McClure a resident of the same city, a Scotchman of wealth, science and liberality also came, and eventually made a large investment in the lands of the community. The celebrated Frances Wright likewise became a member, and Mr. Owen's two sons, Robert Dale, who has been a member of Congress from that district, and is now United States Chargé at Naples, and David Dale who for some years has been the State Geologist of Indiana, and has distinguished himself in surveys for the General Government in the North-west, arrived from Scotland.

Some difficulties in the coalescing and harmonizing of the discordant elements of the new society thus by chance thrown together were experienced; but they were not insurmountable and shortly disappeared. Mr. Owen proposed that the intelligent and moral powers of man should combine with his physical powers in one harmonious effort for the common good. He held that an immediate supply of all the necessaries and comforts of life and a certainty of future supply were indispensible to human happiness, as were, likewise virtue and health; and he maintained that these were best insured in a system where each individual contributes by his exertions to the common stock, as was abundantly proven by the history of the Quakers, the Shakers and the Moravians. No form of religion, nor mode of worship was either prescribed or forbidden. There was perfect toleration. A neat white church of wood, with a spire and two bells rose in the midst of the village, however, where each could worship as he chose. Dogmas and forms of faith were deemed of little value. Morality was maintained by a simple code strictly enforced. "Do to others as you would others should do to you" was at once the motto and mandate of the Society. Enlightened public opinion was deemed the surest corrector and regulator of morals, and "the rejuvenating principle of virtue," in it was held, must ever prove most efficient in communities where each member had a direct interest in the good conduct and industry of each and all. In such a community, though the bad or the idle might gain entrance, they would not long find it for their interest or comfort to remain.

But it was on the education of the young that the projector of the new Social System relied for ultimate success in his plan for the amelioration of the condition of mankind. To re-model characters already formed under the old system of society he had no hope of, and only expected to modify them in some degree by surrounding them with circumstances favourable to goodness. Education, therefore, was viewed as public property and a public right in which every individual had an equal interest. From the age of two years to that of twelve, it was provided that every child in the community should be carefully instructed, educated, reared, trained, boarded and clothed at a public establishment, with a direct view to the new form of society. A large, airy, commodious three-story brick edifice was appropriated for a school, with accommodations for a hundred and sixty children, where all those belonging to the community, more than a hundred in number, were reared and educated at the common cost. Pupils, also, were received from abroad, the entire charge for their education and support including board, lodging, clothing, books, and medical attendance and medicine if sick, being but $100 per annum. The system pursued was similar to that which had obtained at New Lanark, in Scotland. There were no rewards and no penalties. The pupils were taught to prize goodness for its own sake: that virtue was the best policy: that they could be happy only as others were happy; while the intellectual instruction imparted was restricted to the practical and demonstrable, and avoided the abstract and the abstruse. Care was taken also to blend amusement with study among the children, and recreation with work among the adults, and that, too, as an essential element in the economy of life. Every Tuesday night, therefore, there was a general assembly and ball, with music and dancing; every Friday night a concert by an excellent amateur band; every Wednesday night meetings for public debate, and every Sunday meetings to hear moral, philosophical, or religious lectures. The large room on the ground floor of the Town Hall was devoted to balls, concerts, and public meetings; and was lighted for all who chose to make it a rendezvous for reading or conversation every night. The apartments above and in the wings of the same edifice were devoted to music, more private discussion, or social gatherings. Subsequently a theatre was established and conducted by amateur players.

Although the industrial pursuits at New Harmony under Owen's system continued to be chiefly agricultural as they had been under that of Rapp, manufactures and the useful arts were not neglected. One spacious edifice was devoted to the purposes of a Mill, and another to those of a Factory for cotton and wool, the machinery of both being driven by a steam-engine of sixty horse-power. Neither of the communities, however, seem to have availed themselves of the excellent water-privilege. A Brewery, a Tan Yard, a Soap and Candle Factory, and other like establishments were conducted on a large scale, and extensive weaving, dressing and dying houses soon sent forth cloths and flannels in high repute throughout the country. A military legion was also established embracing companies of infantry, artillery, rifles and fusileers, about two hundred and fifty men in all. In the autumn of 1825, a small weekly newspaper under the name of the "New Harmony Gazette" was commenced; and it continued to be conducted with ability and judgment for several years, and even after the virtual dissolution of the community. The editor in the issue of October 29th, 1825, of this little sheet expresses himself not only as sanguine, but as confident of the Society's success. At that time Mr. Owen was absent in England, but his return is duly chronicled on the 12th of January of the ensuing year.

The system at this time seems to have been in a full tide of successful experiment; and the healthiness of the locality may be inferred from the facts recorded in the Gazette, that, during the years 1823 and 1824, out of eight hundred inhabitants, only seven were lost by disease; while, during the six first months of 1825, out of a population of nine hundred, many of whom were children, there were only three deaths, one of which only was of an adult. The spot, however, was not exempt from the remittent fevers of the country, and to this cause, indeed, has been attributed the departure of the Harmonites more than to any other.

Meantime another society, somewhat on the communal system, had been founded by an Englishman named Birkbeck at a place called Albion, in Illinois, on the Little Wabash, and some twenty miles distant from New Harmony. In 1843, a book in which is given the history of Albion, was published in London, written by George Flower, who was an associate of Birkbeck for twenty years, and until the former lost his life by drowning in the Wabash. Mr. Birkbeck was at one time Secretary of State for the State of Illinois, and with Mr. Flower expended large sums in the improvement of their town. Upon the decease of the two founders of the place, its peculiar characteristics of society were resigned, though it continued a thriving town and a great market in a section of country remarkable for fertility and beauty.

The social experiment on the banks of the Wabash excited much curiosity and interest, not only in the United States, but also in Europe; and distinguished philosophers and philanthropists not only corresponded with Mr. Owen to learn his success, but also visited his settlement with the same view. Among these was no less a personage than the Duke of Saxe Weimar, who, while travelling in the West, visited New Harmony in April, 1826, and passed a week there. In his volumes of travels, subsequently published, the Duke gives a detailed account of the mode of living of the society, day by day, at its highest prosperity. The community at this time numbered a thousand members, who took their meals in four large boarding-houses. Two small rooms in other buildings were awarded to each married couple, the smaller children being lodged in the common nursery, and the larger ones being at the common school; while the common kitchen, dining-room and parlour were, as has been seen, elsewhere supplied. The Duke accompanied Mr. Owen to the shops of the shoemakers, joiners, tailors, saddlers and smiths in a building formerly used by the religious Germans for a church; and in each shop were boys receiving instruction in these mechanical arts. He also saw the boys at military exercise, and at their lessons in fencing. The principal avocation of the young girls seemed to be the plaiting of straw hats. On several occasions the Duke was present at public concerts, balls and recitations, and expresses suprise and gratification at the proficiency of the amateur performers. One evening Mr. Owen delivered a lecture on the steam-engine, after which there was a promenade and a quadrille to the music of an excellent band. Sunday morning the whole village assembled in the large apartment of the Town Hall, and, after music by the band, listened to a discourse by Mr. Owen on the advantages of his Social System. The evening was beautiful, and there was an aquatic excursion on the Wabash with music, and subsequently a ball with reels, quadrilles and waltzes, one of the figures being called "The New Social System," though some of the ladies at first objected to "dancing on Sunday." The Duke mentions as a somewhat severe test of practical equality, that a young and pretty girl, who was charming everybody with a sweet song at the piano, was called away at the zenith of her triumph to milk the cows, in doing which she was very unkindly trodden on by one and horned at by another!

The summer costume of the society for the men consisted of white pantaloons buttoned to the lower edge of a jacket without a collar; and that of the women was the regular Bloomer garb of a frock to the knees with pantalets. The Duke thought his friend Say, the naturalist, looked quite comical in his boy's roundabout and breeches; while his hands were blistered with unaccustomed gardening.

Mr. Owen urged on the Duke as the peculiar doctrines of his system perfect equality and fraternity, and entire toleration of religious belief and worship, while he denounced the pledge of everlasting love at the altar as absurd, and explained that in his society children would prove no impediment to the separation of parents, inasmuch as they all belonged to the community from their second year. The benevolent enthusiast was sanguine in the conviction that these principles were destined to reform the whole world—to abolish crime and its penalty—to create identity of interest among all mankind, and, of consequence, to put an end forever to controversy and dissension. And yet, at that very time, and hardly a year from the commencement of his experiment, and in the very youth and hey-day of its fancied triumph, his noble guest could plainly perceive that the seeds of dissension and disunion were already sown, and sown broadcast. Equality was only a name. Fraternity of feeling, or even of association, seemed impossible between the educated and elegant and refined, and the ignorant and vulgar and coarse; and all attempts at it resulted only in disgust and chagrin. Like sought like, and sought like only; and forced fraternity was as disagreeable to the high as the low—to those on one side as to those on the other. Among the men this fraternity was barely possible; but with the women it seemed out of the question, and even the little girls received with ill-concealed disgust the democratic partners which lot bestowed on them in the dance. Indeed, within the first twelvemonth of the society's existence nearly every member declared himself dissatisfied and disappointed, and, while their leader was sanguine of success, could plainly foresee inevitable and speedy dissolution. This conviction became absolute certainty in their minds when on the 4th of July, 1826, being the fiftieth of American independence, their leader put forth his celebrated "Declaration of Mental Independence." In this remarkable document he says, that, inasmuch as at his age the continuance of life was very uncertain, he had calmly and deliberately determined on that eventful and auspicious occasion, "to break asunder the remaining mental bonds which for so many ages had grievously afflicted our nature, and by so doing to give for ever full freedom to the human mind." He then declares to the world, upon an experience of forty years, more varied and extended than had ever before fallen to man's lot, devoted to tracing out the causes of human misery, that "man, up to that hour, had been in all parts of the earth a slave to a trinity the most monstrous that could be combined to inflict mental and physical evil on his whole race"—that trinity consisting of "private or individual property, absurd and irrational systems of religion and marriage, founded on individual property, combined with some one of these systems of religion—a trinity so intimately interlinked and woven together by time, that it could not be separated without being destroyed—

a trinity compounded of ignorance, superstition and hypocrisy, and proving the only devil that ever has or ever would torment the human race—the only cause of all the crime, and all the misery arising from crime, which could be found in human society! The fulness of time for giving the death-blow to this despotism which for ages had held the mind in fetters so mysterious that no mortal had dared to approach them, had at length, the reformer declared, after forty years of preparation and half a century after the political independence of '76 arrived; and he called on his friends to rejoice with him that the irrevocable deed was done—that their mental independence was now as secure as their civil, and that the great truth just promulged would speedily pervade the continent and the globe and wherever conveyed would by the human heart be recognized and received!

It was Tuesday when this oration, the most extraordinary, certainly, of all the extraordinary orations that were ever inflicted on that devoted day—the Fourth of July; and on the ensuing Sunday the orator informed the assembled citizens that it would be published in the Gazette for their careful perusal; and if no error could be found in it, a course of action might be founded on it leading to the Millenium!

The Address was published, and its effects were as speedy as they were inevitable. All prudent people — people of property or family, at once abandoned the society. Those who had wavered in their purpose before wavered now no longer. The die was cast. Mr. Owen, however, seems to have been not at all surprised at the result. Indeed, he appears to have anticipated it, when in the opening of this same address he declares that in view of the immeasurable good which this mental revolution would secure to man throughout all future ages, the continued residence there a little longer of a few individuals was of no consideration whatever. He probably had no idea, however, that in dealing "a death-blow to the old system of society" he was annihilating the experiment of his own, for he closes his address by urging on his hearers to unite their separate interests into one—to abolish all money transactions of an individual character—to exchange with each other articles of produce on the basis of labor for equal labor—to apply surplus wealth to aid others to gain like advantages, and to abandon all use of spirituous liquors.

But, however faithfully the benevolent reformer might preach the propriety of applying surplus wealth to aid others in gaining the same, and however faithfully also he might perform the more difficult task of practising what he preached, he was not so foolish as to waste his substance in supporting the dissolute and idle, a task which very shortly alone remained to him. The ensuing year, therefore, saw the end of his experiment and his return to England, having disposed of a portion of his houses and lands at great loss, to Mr. McClure, already mentioned, for $50,000. His family remained however, retaining possession of most of the original estate, and have there continued ever since to reside.

In the spring of 1830, three or four years after these events, Mr. Stewart, an English traveller, visited the spot, and pronounced it one of the most attractive he had seen in America. He said he was struck with the gay aspect of the place even before the boat moved from the western bank to take him over. It was a beautiful Sunday evening, and the whole population of the village seemed to be in the open air. In a few minutes he had crossed the stream, and found himself in an excellent hotel with that rare convenience in the West, a good reading room. The houses, enclosures and grounds were, at that time, a mere wreck of what they had been in the time of Rapp. On the dissolution of the Society, some wanton depredations had been perpetrated on the property by some of those ill-disposed persons who had viewed the philanthropic reformer as only a lawful prey, so long as he would submit to their plunderings and the first object of their vengeance and ingratitude when he would do so no longer. The orchard, vineyard and garden of a hundred acres cultivated originally by Rapp, still seemed well kept, however; the roads and walks around the place were most inviting; and Mr. Stewart concludes by saying, that "Harmony certainly still continued to be a place which every traveller in the western country of America ought to see," and which were it as healthy as it was beautiful, would prove a most delightful and desirable residence. The Duke of Saxe Weimar's pretty girl who had been called from the piano to the milk-pail to exemplify equality and industry, was then a happy wife and mother. The population was still some six hundred; but made up as it was of adventurers from all parts of the Union and the world, it was deemed "extremely demoralised." Some excellent families still remained, however, and of those who departed, many even to this day look back on the few years passed at New Harmony, as the happiest of their lives. The Society certainly left its impress on the place, and its population is far more intelligent and refined than most other towns of its size in the West. Its population is now about one thousand. All the log cabins of the Germans have disappeared, and it is the seat of justice for Posey County.

The great error of Mr. Owen in carrying out his system, independently of any errors in the system itself, has been deemed by all who have expressed an opinion on the subject, to have been his indiscriminate reception of persons to membership, regardless of character, habits, prejudices, nationalities, civil or religious creeds, or prior private life and reputation. Thus, while many of those who came to New Harmony were persons of industry and intelligence, probity and property, and sincerely desirous of giving the new system for the amelioration of the manifold and palpable evils of society a fair trial, others were idle, dissolute, needy and unprincipled adventurers, who sought the place only as the readiest mode of obtaining the best living with the least exertion, and, in fact, only to be supported by Mr. Owen and his worthy associates in idleness and ease. Had all who sought this new Arcadia on the banks of the Wabash, been alike only in education, refinement and property, though dissimilar in dispositions, habits, tastes, nationalities and prior associations, there might have been some hope of ultimate amalgamation; but as it was, dissension, discord, disunion and dissolution were as speedy as they were unavoidable.

About the time of the visit of Mr. Stewart to New Harmony, it was visited also by Mr. Flower, the associate of Mr. Birkbeck in his settlement at Albion, who, in his work subsequently published, already named, speaks of the attempted Utopias of Rapp and Owen—of Zeno and Epicurus—of the Portico and the Garden as having been commenced with equally high hopes—sustained with equally great efforts, and as having equally and signally failed—both experiments, like all others of the kind before or since, seeming to prove such systems entirely practicable, while the fruition of full success is forever deferred—being always just successful enough to induce others to follow their example.

In the spring of 1843, New Harmony was visited by Mr. Dean, who writes in the "New Moral World," that there remained there "not the least semblance of a community." One of the large brick edifices of the Germans was appropriated to a "Working Man's Institute," of which there were some sixty members, and before which Robert and David Dale Owen occasionally lectured on scientific topics. Its library numbered four hundred volumes, and Mr. McClure had a library, also, containing twice the number, of which he was very liberal. There was, likewise, a Museum and a Theatre, and the population was about four hundred. Sheep and stock were abundant—"hog and hominy" were the common fare, and large quantities of produce were sent off on flat-boats every spring to New Orleans, some twelve hundred miles distant. It was about this time, probably, that Prince Maximilian of Neuwied, passed some weeks at the place with his party of naturalists, during which the Prince exercised his graceful pencil in delineating several of the romantic scenes in the neighborhood. One of these in the Fox Island Cut-off, is exceedingly picturesque, as is also that of the village itself.

In the spring of 1846, Sir Charles Lyell visited David Dale Owen, and passed with him several days. He found at New Harmony many intelligent English and Swiss families living comfortably but simply and with great sociality. There were many private parties, and a public assembly was held once each week supplied with music by the amateur band. Sir Charles was charmed with the happy, merry, and perfectly obedient children he found here, and alludes to "the singular phenomenon in America of a *shy child*" found by him only at New Harmony. Another singular phenomenon observed by him was the absence of a church; and still a third the absence of a grog-shop! Dr. Owen's Museum afforded the Baronet much satisfaction. This extensive collection of minerals and fossils has been chiefly made by Dr. Owen in his geological surveys for the State of Indiana and the General Government, and he has a fine laboratory for analysis and experiment. The old Granary of the Rappites, which a few years since was presented to him by Miss McClure, is now appropriated to this museum, as already mentioned. New Harmony is still the residence of all the family of the old reformer, consisting of Robert Dale Owen, U. S. Chargé d' Affaires at Naples, Dr. David Dale Owen, State Geologist of Indiana, Major Richard Owen, and Mrs. Jane Fauntleroy. Robert Owen is still living in England, and though above eighty years old, still preaches the reform of the world by his New Social System. On the 4th of August, 1844, on the eve of rejoining his family in America after an absence of ten years, "being in good health of body and mind," he issued from Rose Hill his "Second Legacy to the Human Race," some eighteen years since the promulgation of his celebrated "Declaration of Mental Independence" at New Harmony, on the 4th of July, 1826. In this latter document, scarcely less extraordinary than the former, he declares as the result of nearly sixty years' investigation and experience that happiness for the human race is possible and may be permanent and progressive: that all must be happy or none: that enlightened equality is indispensible, and that general information is essential to this equality: that no one was so capable of giving advice on this subject as the testator; that the world had hitherto been, and still was governed by force and fraud, by priests and despots: that every existence desires happiness and seeks it according to its knowledge, there being no merit in the thing in man or brute, and that, consequently, there is no merit or demerit in the governments or the priesthood in governing mankind by force and fraud, their instinctive desire for happiness compelling them to act thus: that mankind may be governed by reason and affection as well as by force and fraud, that the former would most conduce to happiness; but to overturn the old system would result in much evil, and the benefit would be slow though for the interest of all: that man is a creature of circumstances, and may be improved by their improvement: that the governors and priests by their acts of omission and commission are the real cause through their ignorance of all the disease crime and suffering, or the sin and misery of the human race: that the great trinity of evils is Private Property, Superstition and Formal Marriage: that relief is to be gained only by complete abandonment of this trinity and its causes; and that its result would be society regenerated, wealth abundant, peace permanent, knowledge universal, the earth highly and wholly cultivated, the arts and sciences flourishing, health and happiness, charity and love abounding, and the inferior qualities of men gradually disappearing. This extraordinary paper thus concludes:—"This is my second and may be my last legacy; and if so, I call on all friends of progress to cherish it in their minds, to consider it again and again; for it contains the words of TRUTH, without mystery, mixture of error, or fear of man."

DRAWN AFTER NATURE. For the Proprietor: HERRMANN J. MEYER.

St. CHARLES on the MISSISSIPPI

Published for HERRMANN J. MEYER. 164, William-Str. NEW-YORK.

ST. CHARLES.

The time was, and it has not long passed, when the old French village of St. Charles was deemed one of the outposts of civilization. It was here that hunters, trappers, *engagés and coureurs du bois* were found by the American Fur Company for their trade to the Rocky Mountains; here expeditions to Santa Fe were fitted out, and this was the point of their final departure; and here was the home of many of the *voyageurs* and boatmen to whom thirty years ago was committed the navigation of the western waters. St. Charles was the rendezvous, also, of the Indian tribes when they visited the settlements, and was long the capital of Missouri. For these reasons and for others, St. Charles was, at one time, and for a considerable period, one of the most important places in the Far West; and is, therefore, independently of its antiquity, its origin, and the beauty of its site, deserving of extended notice.

St. Charles is one of those villages founded by the followers of La Salle and their descendants on the great rivers of the West, which constitute such a striking feature in its history, and the characteristics of which, after the lapse of more than a century, are so remarkably retained. Among these villages may be named Kaskaskia and Cahokia founded in 1683, and Peoria, Prairie du Rocher, Prairie du Pont, Portage des Sioux, St. Phillipe, St. Genevieve, St. Ferdinand, now Florissant, Vide Poche, now Carondelet, Pain Court, now St. Louis, and Les Petites Cotes, now St. Charles, founded at different periods. The last named place was settled by French Canadians in 1769, six years after the founding of St. Louis by Laclede, or, as others say, not until 1780, and owed its original name, which it retained for more than forty years, to the heights by which it is overlooked. Subsequently it was named St. Andrews and finally St. Charles. For some years after Missouri became a State, St. Charles was the capital, and it so continued until October, 1826, when the seat of government was removed to the city of Jefferson, farther up the Missouri. It was also the territorial capital, and here sat the Convention in 1820 which framed the present constitution—that constitution which caused a conflict so fierce in the United States Congress, and a sensation so profound throughout the country.

To the early French rule over all this territory succeeded that of Spain; but, by the treaty of St. Ildefonso, France resumed her sway, and that of the United States followed. The first commandant of St. Charles was Pierre Blanchett. To him succeeded Charles Tayon; and James Mackay was her ruler at the time of the cession to the United States. During the War of 1812–15 with Great Britain, and during Indian hostilities both before and after, the town and county of St. Charles suffered terribly from savage atrocities. As one of the advanced settlements on our extended frontier it was the scene of fearful outrage on one side and intrepid courage on the other. Whole tribes of savages came pouring down from the northwestern wilderness—the Iowas, Miamies, Pottawattamies, Kickapoos, Sacs and Foxes,—on the defenceless settlers; and the same horrors and the same bravery were beheld, as under the same circumstances, at an earlier period, on the "Dark and Bloody Ground" of Kentucky. The Federal Government, being unable to afford protection to its boundless frontier, the settlers were forced to protect themselves, and, forming themselves into bands called "Rangers," and constructing stockades and block-houses as retreats for their women and children, for more than two years they maintained incessant warfare, and performed some of the most brilliant feats which distinguish American history during that sanguinary and unnatural strife. At a subsequent period, in the absence of efficient government, the "Rangers," who had been the protectors in time of war, became "Regulators," who maintained law and order against the evil disposed by summary and, perchance, salutary chastisement of notorious offenders,—in much the same manner, it may be remarked, as did perhaps, the celebrated Secret Tribunals of Westphalia during the Middle Ages.

The site of St. Charles is a bed of secondary limestone, and it is the last one found descending the Missouri. Between this point and the *embouchure* into the Mississippi, a distance of twenty-five miles, there is only alluvion on the western bank, while, on the eastern, the bluffs of La Charboniere and Bellefontaine prevent the mighty stream from cutting across the point and seeking its rival five miles above St. Louis instead of twenty. From St. Louis to St. Charles across this point is but twenty miles; while by the detour of the rivers it is more than twice that distance. Directly opposite St. Charles, between the river and the bluffs, extends a strip of bottom-land a mile or two broad, clothed with enormous trees and vines, the black alluvion deeply buried in the sands of repeated inundations. The inroads of the river during the past thirty years on this yielding soil have been alarming. Where once stood cottages, gardens, orchards, farms, whole forests of enormous sycamores, now roll the turbid waters of the giant flood.

Above St. Charles the furious stream has been yet more devastating, and the site of the town of Franklin, one of the oldest in the State, some twenty years ago was completely swept away.

In many respects the Missouri is the most extraordinary stream on the globe. For the caprices and violence of its current, for the vast quantities of soil with which its waters are charged, it is not less remarkable than for its enormous volume and its endless course. Rising in the Chippewa Range of the Rocky Mountains, within a few miles of the Columbia, the great river of the Pacific, it rushes forth through its adamantine portal, fifty yards wide, six miles long, and more than twice the height of the Hudson Highlands at West Point, on either side, upon the vast plains of the farthest West. The Yellow Stone and the White rivers pour into it their turbid torrents—the Kansas, the Platte, the Osage, and hundreds of lesser streams contribute their respective quotas, until, at length, swollen to monster dimensions, it disgorges itself into the clear and sparkling waters of the Mississippi, and the character of the latter stream is changed forever. From the savage nations on its banks it bore the name indifferently of "The Smoky Water," "The Mad River," "The Mother of Floods," each significant of its distinctive features. Its turbid character is attributed to the sand and clay of its tributaries, though it is said to be almost as turbid before receiving their contributions, as after; and, still more strange, its volume at St. Charles, like that of the Mississippi at New Orleans, seems hardly greater, after receiving all these floods into its bosom, than before, a thousand miles above. Superior to its rival in extent and volume, it is inferior in the wealth of its valley, and the directions of its course; and fails, therefore, to give its name to that joint stream to which it nevertheless so decidedly imparts its character. Its navigation, owing to the violence of its current, the variableness of its channel, and the number and variety of its obstructions, is the most perilous of all western rivers; the wages of pilots and hands, and the rates of freight and insurance, are higher on its waters than on those of any other western stream; which, on most of its course, steamers do not venture to ascend at night. More power in machinery and more strength in construction are, also, demanded by boats designed for this trade, than for any other in the West. At first, indeed, steam-power ample to stem the Mississippi was found entirely inefficient for its more furious rival. In the summer of 1819, a government expedition up the Missouri to the Yellow Stone entirely failed, because the steamers provided, after toiling against the current for weeks, were forced to resign all idea of overcoming it. Every exertion was made, but the current was too violent for the steamers then constructed, and the loss to government from the failure was great. Only one boat, a small one of a hundred tons, named "Western Engineer," succeeded in ascending to Council Bluffs; she was constructed at Pittsbugh expressly for the purpose. She was very strong, had a powerful engine, a stern-wheel, and was commanded by Captain Long, now stationed at Louisville, and Colonel of Topographical Engineers. She was armed and manned against assaults from savage tribes; but the savages were too much terrified by the *Pinelore* — the fire-canoe — as they called the monster, to approach her. And well they might be. Her escape-pipe terminated in the head of a huge serpent, and protruding from the prow, instead of ascending from the hurricane-roof, at every revolution of her wheels, belched forth a volume of steam, with a roar that made the forests ring, while her blazing furnaces flung their red glare over the turbid wave. Next year, the fall of 1820, Capt. Pierce of Cincinnati, had constructed three strong and powerful stern-wheel boats, and went to St. Louis, with the hope of securing the contract to take the United States stores to Council Bluffs at four dollars the hundred; but he was underbid by Col. Richard M. Johnson, who proposed to take them up at three dollars and a third per hundred, but utterly failed, the power of his boats proving insufficient.

The current of the Missouri averages four miles an hour, while that of the Mississippi averages but three. It is navigable two thousand miles above the confluence, while the Mississippi is navigable less than one. Its annual flood is in June, some weeks later than that of its rival, the melted snows at the sources of the former having a less distance to flow and a more direct route to pursue; and thus the inundation and devastation of the united floods are avoided. The proportion of sediment with which its waters are charged is estimated at one-third its volume. They, also, hold in solution sulpher and nitre, and are cathartic in tendency to those unaccustomed to drink them. They are, however, deemed not only salubrious, but even specifically remedial in cutaneous diseases; and are decidedly preferred by the dwellers on their banks, despite their cloudy aspect, to the purest spring water that can be procured. Pumice stone, which is constantly found floating in the Missouri or reposing on its bars and islands, would seem to indicate the existence of an active volcano at some point along its extended course.

The town of St. Charles stretches along a narrow *plateau* a distance of more than a mile, and up the hill-side of the sloping bluffs some hundreds of feet in altitude. It has been laid off into streets parallel with the river, five in number, intersected by others at right angles, at intervals of two or three hundred feet. But one of these streets, however—that along the river-bank—the "Main Street" of the village, exhibits much activity. Indeed, this street constitutes St. Charles, and quite as much now as half a century ago. Here are the stores, here the taverns and groceries, here the mart and gathering-spot of the whole town. The street is perfectly level, is macadamized and bordered on either sides by paved side-walks, a luxury by the by, which no other of these ancient places, except St. Louis, can boast. A prominent feature of Main Street is a huge steam flouring mill of stone on the margin of the river, which, night and day, for twenty odd years, Sundays only excepted, has been sending forth its everlasting and monotonous puff. Among the houses are beheld relics of French and Spanish taste and domination in heavy-roofed, broad-galleried cottages of logs chinked, plastered and whitewashed, now in ruins; but the number is few and is annually growing less. Along the hill-side and upon the bluffs are sprinkled structures, among which, on the summit, is beheld St. Charles College with its cupola, an imposing edifice of stone. Conspicuous, also, on this eminence is a round tower of stone, to which, as a sort of land-mark in history, no little interest attaches. Originally it was constructed as a fort and magazine, during Spanish domination, half a century since, like a structure of the same character on the bank of the Mississippi in North St. Louis, which has now disappeared, known as "Roy's Tower." Its masonry is massive, its walls two or three feet thick, its diameter about a dozen feet, and its altitude some twenty or thirty. During Indian hostilities, the old tower doubtless played its part as an outpost, vidette or place of retreat, and subsequently presented a foundation for a windmill. But it seems to have been no more successful in its new vocation, than similar contrivances in other parts of the West, and was ere long abandoned to time and the elements. The old pile is now but a monument of the past, and, also, a monument of a solitary grave which lies near its base. It is the last resting place, at his own desire, of a young man named Barton, a lawyer of St. Louis who, some thirty years ago, was slain in a duel by a political opponent named Collier, on Bloody Island, in the Mississippi, opposite the city. This is not the only fatal rencontre of this character witnessed by that desolate spot. It was here that Farrar slew Graham, here that Benton slew Lucas, here that Pettis and Biddle slew each other; while the less fatal or altogether bloodless combats witnessed by its sterile sands have been quite numberless.

The College at St. Charles owes its origin and establishment to an old lady of the place, Mrs. Catharine Collier, by whom the main edifice had been nearly completed in 1835, when she died. Her benevolent design was, however, carried out by her son, George Collier, who was born at St. Charles, and there began accumulating that large fortune, in commercial avocations, which subsequently distinguished him as a merchant of St. Louis. In August of 1835, the institution was opened by three teachers, and for several succeeding years was sustained by its patron. It was then incorporated as a College, a Board of Curators from the Missouri Conference of the Methodist Church were appointed, and the property was assigned to their control, an endowment of $1,000 per annum being settled upon it by Mr. Collier. Liberal donations have since been made to the institution by other members of the Methodist Church, by whom it has been mainly sustained, and furnished with a library and laboratory. It is calculated with its appurtenances to accommodate more than a hundred students, and has some half dozen professorships. The President from its earliest foundation has been the Rev. John H. Fielding. The institution has never become celebrated and probably never will; but its healthful and retired location, its judicious discipline, the respectable position of its faculty, and the sound instruction it is able to impart will always render it a valuable school of the Methodist Church. Its prominent patron, Mr. Collier, died a few years ago, one of the wealthiest men in St. Louis; and, unlike most *millionaires*, he was as liberal as he was opulent, and deserves to rank ever with the merchant-princes of the Athens of the North, for his charitable, religious and educational endowments.

The Catholics, also, of St. Charles have their institutions for instruction. The Sisters of the Convent of the Sacred Heart conduct a Seminary for Young Ladies, and there is a large school for boys superintended by Priests. Churches are somewhat numerous, the Catholics and Lutherans worshipping in edifices of stone, and the Presbyterians and Methodists in structures of brick. The Catholics outnumber the Protestants at St. Charles, although the proportion of the latter is much greater in this than in any other of these old places of French origin, St. Louis only excepted. By the terms of the charter of the town, the municipal rule is reposed in the hands of a Board of Seven Trustees, by whom all appointments to office are made.

The view of St. Charles from the hurricane-roof of a Western steamer, ascending or descending the Missouri, is imposing and picturesque. Its site is elevated and healthy; its population about two thousand; its manufacturing facilities considerable; the soil in its vicinity and in the county of which it is the seat of justice, unsurpassed in fertility; the farms extensive and highly cultivated, and productive of excellent wheat; the quarries of rock, beds of coal, and forests of timber, are exhaustless; immigration, especially of Germans, is constant and heavy; and, if a continuation of circumstances like this can conduce to prosperity, St. Charles bids fair to become a flourishing and important place.

Above St. Charles, the bed of lime-rock which is the site of the town shortly terminates, and is succeeded by a bottom heavily timbered; while below, it terminates in alluvion, which stretches along beneath the bluffs some two or three miles, until reaching the point where the highlands of the Missouri meet with those of the Mississippi, it expands into the cultivated Prairie of the Mamelles. This prairie takes its name from a couple of lofty bluffs which are formed by the junction of the highlands, and which bear a striking resemblance to a woman's breast. The view from the summit of these swelling and graceful eminences is unsurpassed in beauty. On the left go off the bluffs, sometimes approaching the Mississippi in bold and naked crags, but, as a general thing, sweeping away some four or five miles from the belt of heavy timber which rises along its banks. On the right flows the Missouri with its range of bluffs on the opposite side, and its flourishing farms on the bottom at your feet, while in front is spread out the vast and beautiful Mamelle Prairie, more than fifty thousand acres, at a single glance, bounded by the fringe of forest along the Mississippi, and the white cliffs along the Illinois shore beyond.

The Mamelle Prairie in many respects resembles the American Bottom. From Alton to the mouth of the Illinois there rise from the water a range of castellated cliffs, like those of Selma and Herculaneum below St. Louis, while, in each instance, on the opposite bank spreads out a broad bottom to the bluffs beyond. Both bottoms, also, embrace several lakes of considerable extent, as well as numerous lagunes; and from the depths of the alluvion in either locality have been disinterred logs of wood, lumps of mineral coal, and strata of pebbles and sand. That both of these vast meadows were once the bed of a lake, seems hardly doubtful; while the cause of that vast water-sheet, some two hundred miles in length by five or six in breadth, seems indicated by the remains of a gigantic parapet of lime-stone, more than a hundred feet high, which once dammed the waters of the Mississippi below St. Louis.

The confluence of the two great rivers takes place thirty miles from the Mamelles. The bottom runs off to a low point clothed with enormous trees. About a dozen miles above, on the Mississippi, stands the old French village of Prairie des Sioux. Buried in the rank luxuriance of gigantic vegetation, and seemingly isolated from all the world beside, it is more than thirty miles from St. Louis, six or eight from Alton and five or six from the mouth of the Illinois, while, nearly opposite, sheer and stark, go up from the water's edge the white Piasan cliffs below Grafton. The place is nearly surrounded by enormous forest-trees. It exhibits all the peculiarities of the other villages of the same origin. Each broad-roofed and galleried cottage is surrounded by its garden plat; a few narrow lanes are the only thoroughfares; it has a common-field of twelve hundred acres stretching out into the Point Prairie, a few hundred inhabitants, a few stores, a safe landing for steamers and an old Catholic church. The place was settled more than half a century since by villagers from old Cahokia, and many of its cottages suffered severely from the celebrated earthquakes of the summer of 1811 which nearly destroyed New Madrid. Its peculiar name is said to have originated in a stratagem of a band of Sioux Indians on a hostile expedition against the Missouries who then inhabited the Mamelle Prairie, and whose principal village was the present site of St. Charles. Indeed this fertile and beautiful region seems to have been a favorite residence of the aboriginal inhabitants, if any inference may be drawn from the large quantities of remains of pottery and other utensils thrown up by the ploughshare. The Missouries were at war with the Sioux; and, to anticipate an attack on their principal village designed by their savage foe, all the warriors repaired to the confluence of the rivers, and lay in ambush to assail the enemy as he doubled the point. But the wily Sioux in apprehension of such a stratagem, instead of descending the Mississippi to the confluence as was expected, landed at the Portage above, and bearing their canoes on their backs across the prairie, again entered them in the Missouri, and ascended to the devoted village. Thus taken by surprise, women, children and old men were massacred without mercy, and the plundered lodges were given to the flames. Then secretly and swiftly returning to the confluence, the victorious Sioux fell on the unsuspecting Missouries in their ambuscade, and slaughtered them almost to a man! And thus was the once powerful tribe of the Missouries extinguished. The spot where the exterminating foe landed and over which they bore their canoes has from that day well been termed the Portage des Sioux; for the name is recorded in the blood of a murdered race.

Drawn after nature

For the Proprietor: Herrmann J. Meyer.

BURLINGTON

ON THE MISSISSIPPI.

Published for HERRMANN J. MEYER. 164. William-Str. NEW-YORK.

BURLINGTON, IOWA.

As we pass down the Mississippi towards Burlington, the river changes its appearance; long, low islands, covered with timber, brushwood and creeping vines, divide the channel, and the bluffs are frequently seen on either side, at some distance beyond the alluvial bottom lands. On both sides beyond the ridge of bluffs, lies a fertile country, over which, at intervals, farms have been cleared. Much of the land yet lies in a state of nature. The timber increases as we descend the river, and beautifully undulating prairies lie between the water courses. Along the western side, between the river and the bluffs, is an extensive tract of low alluvial land, full of lakes and marshes, extending to Flint Hills. As we turn through a bend of the river, the city of Burlington is presented in view.

This is an incorporated city, and the largest in the State of Iowa, having in 1852, more than 6000 inhabitants. The site is admirable, and the streets and buildings ascend from the border of the river up the slope of the bluff to the table land in the rear. From the opposite shore, or in ascending or descending the river, the view is highly picturesque. A large part of the city lies in the form of an amphitheatre, along the surrounding hills, while another portion spreads over the plateau in the back ground. Neat buildings and cottages have been erected here, and on the streets and elevated ground in the rear. Churches for several religious denominations shoot forth their spires above the other buildings, while a spacious court house for Des Moines county may be seen on an elevated site. A college for the Baptist denomination is to be established on the high ground in the vicinity, and the erection of a building for it has been commenced. The city has good schools, both public and private.

Burlington is conveniently situated to command the trade of an extensive and fertile agricultural region on both sides of the Mississippi, and for a short period it was the seat of the territorial government of Wisconsin, and then of Iowa Territory, from the period of its separate organization, until 1840. It is 245 miles above St. Louis, and 95 miles below Rock Island.

The eminences along the western side of the Mississippi, both above and below this city were called *Shok-o-quan* by the Indians, and Flint Hills by Americans. A trading house was kept here many years before the pale faces and civilization came into this region, and to this spot the aborigines resorted to barter their furs and peltry for the goods of the white men, and drink the fire-water that laid many a brawny savage in a premature grave. In excavating cellars and grading streets, laboring men throw up the mouldering remains of a departed race, and the war-club, tomahawk, stone pipe, and other appendages of an Indian burial are found here. Yet Shok-o-quan was not the site of any large Indian town. No aborigines were here, or seen along the river from Wisconsin to the lower rapids of the Mississippi, when Marquette and Joliet passed down in 1673. The country of Iowa was originally claimed by the *Aiouez* of the French journalists, or Ioways. They were driven off west, and their country taken from them by the Sauks and Foxes, in the early part of the eighteenth century, and the whole territory along the Mississippi remained in possession of these Indians, until the close of the Black Hawk war in 1832. A strip of country fifty miles wide was then ceded to the United States. There was a small tract at Dubuque, including lead mines, that had been purchased by a previous treaty, where a frontier village of miners and traders had sprung up. On no other part of the territory could any persons settle but licensed traders, and others who had authority from the government. The general impression that prevailed was, that the Iowa country was one interminable prairie, and could not be inhabited within this century.

In the spring of 1833, farmers from Illinois and other states, with their families, crossed the Mississippi at Shok-o-quan, to turn up the virgin soil, and become the founders of a new state. The country immediately in the rear of the Flint Hills, was undulating, rich, and had a due proportion of timber and prairie. The red man had hardly set his face towards the setting sun, before a hundred families, with their flocks and herds, were "squatters" along the margin of the prairies, in this part of Iowa. No government existed on that side of the Great river, but as in other like cases, they were a "law unto themselves." Good order was maintained spontaneously, and no depredations were committed. Hospitality and kind feelings prevailed, until Congress at the close of a session, attached the whole country, with Wisconsin, to the Territory of Michigan. The Black Hawk Purchase, was then the El Dorado of the far west.

During that season, on all the thoroughfares that crossed the peninsula of the Illinois and Mississippi rivers, emigrants might have been seen in caravans wending their way to the "Purchase." There was much suffering amongst these hardy pioneers, until they could enclose farms and raise crops. Corn for bread could not be obtained, even at an extravagant price, within fifty and even one hundred miles. Those families that had no money to purchase, and teams to haul it that distance, had no alternative but to live without bread until they prepared the ground and cultivated the crop. Their rifles procured meat, and in the autumn honey was to be found in the hollow trees of the forest.

The same spring, (1833,) M. M. McCarver and S. S. White, with their families, built log cabins and lived on the present site of Burlington. The next autumn Messrs. White and A. Doolittle, surveyed the town plot. Lots were sold, emigrants came, and within a few months a village sprang up. Its growth has been steady and rapid, and it is now a place of much business, and the largest city on the right bank of the Mississippi above St. Louis.

PRAIRIE DU ROCHER.

A DOZEN miles north of the old French village of Kaskaskia, on the route to St. Louis, the lofty bluffs which bound the American bottom on the east protrude boldly into the plain, to within three miles of the Mississippi. Abrupt and bald goes up this rocky promontory to the altitude of nearly two hundred feet. From base to summit the face of the cliff bears evidence of having been subjected for centuries to the abrasion of rushing waters. Indeed, so palpable are the phenomena, that the brow of the crag overhangs the base more than a dozen feet, while the same floods which have scooped out the latter into a cave, have chronicled their history in a cornice of parallel grooves of almost architectural uniformity high up on the latter. The cliff is crowned with a thin growth of stunted cedars which bow their heads to the breeze, yet defy the blast, while a few hundred yards up the steep declivity in the rear is encountered a forest of gigantic oaks. Like all the bluffs of the American bottom, this crag is composed of secondary limestone abounding with marine and other petrifactions—madrepores, corallines, concholites and organic remains. The view from the summit is extensive and beautiful. Away on the right is beheld the devious route to Kaskaskia, winding through groves glowing with wild fruit of every species, and common fields carpeted with the emerald tobacco or castor-bean, or waving in rank luxuriance with maize. In front, the course of the Mississippi is traced by the forests of huge sycamores which belt its banks, and the white cliffs which rise on its opposite shore; on the right sweeps off the broad common-field and the broader prairie beyond sprinkled with farms and island-groves; while directly at your feet are scattered along beneath the bluffs the broad-roofed, broad-galleried cottages, the stockade enclosures, the narrow lanes and the luxuriant gardens which constitute an ancient French village of the Mississippi—the village of Prairie du Rocher. The nucleus of this village lies, to be

Drawn after nature

For the Proprietor: HERRMANN J. MEYER.

PRAIRIE DU ROCHER

Published for HERRMANN J. MEYER. 164. William-Street. NEWYORK.

sure, around the little church, two miles above; yet its suburbs may be said to continue for two miles below. The village takes its name from the *rocks* which overhang it. Beneath the shadow of the crag, at its northern base, is beheld an old cottage; while in front a small creek, which has descended through a ravine in the bluffs, winds gracefully on beneath drooping branches, and the arches of a rustic bridge, through the village, and through the bottom, on its way to the river. The cottage is called Barbean's Cottage from its owner's name, and the creek is called Barbean's Creek from the name of the cottage.

It is this point that our artist has selected for his view; and surely a more picturesque, peaceful and beautiful scene can hardly be conceived amid the sunny beauty of a summer day.

"The long sunny lapse of a summer day light."

Yet this romantic spot was once a scene of violence and blood. At that early period when territorial jurisdiction was first extended over this region, and justice was administered by an itinerant court and bar, who, with their libraries and briefs in their saddle-bags, travelled from one point to another, riding the circuit and holding their sessions, the whole cavalcade of legal functionaries, one autumnal afternoon, passing from Cahokia to Kaskaskia, halted their horses to suffer them to drink at Barbean's Creek. The day was sultry, the shade inviting, the stream sparkling and cool: but, hardly had the animals begun to quench their thirst when a volley of rifle shots from the thick shrubbery that skirted the banks, stretched three of the party in blood on the ground! Indians at that period were numerous throughout this region. Remnants of the Kaskaskia tribe still lingered, and the Kickapoos were so hostile to the new American comers, that, in travelling, the disguise of the French villager's garb was almost indispensable to safety. This precaution had been neglected, and the result had been the bloody catastrophe named. The road from Cahokia to Kaskaskia passes over the bridge and directly beneath the beetling crag which affords a welcome shelter from the summer storm.

But the spot is not restricted to tragic associations. It is related of a certain French villager named Pierre Morceau, that, one day, being pursued by a Kaskaskia Indian named Motty, whom he had defrauded in some transaction of peltry, rushed to the brow of the impending crag, and as the sole salvation for life, leaped into the branches of the huge sycamore below. Now, Pierre had, it seems, invested his ill-gotten peltry in a new pair of buckskins, with which, that day, for the first time, he had indued his nether limbs; and, dropping from branch to branch in his headlong course a projecting fork at length pierced the posterior parts of the said integuments, and thus he hung! But Motty had no idea of killing his old friend; and so having pelted him with pebbles until the tough skin of his breeches gave way, he suffered him to crawl off unharmed, bating a few bruises and scratches, to his own cottage. In a few days Pierre re-appeared almost as good as new—thanks to his thrifty helpmate—*almost* as good as new, both breeches and man—but not quite. On the left flank of the unlucky, yet most lucky indispensibles, appeared a piece of old cloth, or rather a piece of old buck-skin,—in the new garment "which was not as before." The rent was not made worse, to be sure; but it told a tale on Pierre, which, by help of Motty's annotations, soon laughed him out of the village; and under the name of "Broken Breeches" he repaired to the little hamlet of Vide Poche, now Carondelet, on the other side of the river, where he lived to a good old age surrounded by descendants.

Prairie du Rocher is, probably, an offshoot of Cahokia or Kaskaskia, and, no doubt, is nearly as old. It was never, however, a much more considerable place than now; and in aspect must be much what it was a hundred years ago. Its population may be a score or two less, though it can hardly be a score or two more. The little weather-beaten old church, which for years received the village worshippers, was consecrated to St. Sulpice, and was, in its palmy day, Chapel of Ease to Fort Chartres, a few miles distant. This celebrated fortress is situated so near Prairie du Rocher, and is so closely allied to it in history that a description of one seems altogether incomplete without some notice of the other.

As early as 1684–5, the chivalric La Salle on visiting Paris after his exploration of the Mississippi and founding the villages of Cahokia and Kaskaskia, urged on Colbert, then at the head of government, the policy of a cordon of military posts from the St. Lawrence to the Gulf of Mexico, a distance of four thousand miles through the wilderness, along the banks of the Ohio and Mississippi, in order to protect the colonies of France in the great valley against the hostile savages, as well as against the colonies of England along the Atlantic coast. The project was favorably viewed, and in furtherance of the scheme, La Salle was to found a colony at the mouth of the Mississippi as a starting point, in prosecution of which enterprise he was assailed by two of his men in the wilderness, and slain. A colony was subsequently founded at this point, and in 1699 the landing of D'Iberville with his Spaniards was strenuously resisted. It was not, however, until thirty or forty years later, when the eyes of all Europe had been directed to Louisiana as the El Dorado of the Western Continent, that the original policy of Colbert began to be carried out. In 1712 Louisiana was farmed out to Crozat for twelve years; but in 1717 he transferred the privilege to John Law's famous "Company of the West," who, for the protection of exhaustless mines of silver and gold, of which the site was supposed to be the peculiar centre, caused the erection of Fort Chartres in 1720. A dozen years later, however, the "Mississippi Bubble" having burst, and Law having retired to Venice to die, the fortress, together with the territory it protected, returned to the Crown. This was in 1731. Twenty-five years afterwards, in 1756, it was re-modeled, re-built and enlarged, and formed one of the chain of fortresses which connected New Orleans with Quebec. There were, at least, a dozen of these posts, whose sites can now be pointed out, one of them, DuQuesne, being at the mouth of the Alleghany, another at the mouth of the Kentucky, a third at the mouth of the Ohio, and others on the Mississippi and Illinois. But of all these fortresses that of Fort Chartres was the most massive as well as the most extensive—indeed, it has been deemed "the best built fort in North America." The material was brought from the bluffs across a lake, and from the opposite shore of the Mississippi. The masonry was so solid, that the tooth of time, and the corrosion of the elements for more than half a century have failed to demolish it. Its original site was the river-bank. In 1721 Charlevoix found it a musket-shot distant from the water; in 1756 a whole mile intervened; in 1766 only eighty paces; in 1722 two of its bastions were undermined by a flood, and, at this present writing, a deep belt of sycamores separates it from the stream. The form of the fort was an irregular quadrangle with four bastions—the sides being some five hundred feet long; with a ditch and scarp; with walls fifteen feet high and two thick, of stone covered with mortar; with ports for cannon and loop-holes for musketry; with mansions for officers—barracks—magazines—prisons—and, indeed, with every appliance, convenience and defence, pertaining to the most finished fortresses of the time. It seems incredible that a structure of such massive and needless strength should, at such immense expense, have been constructed simply against the savages; yet such was the object; and very few are the tens of thousands of voyagers who ascend the Mississippi on the splendid steamers of the present day, who are aware of the fact, that exactly midway between the town of Herculanum and the town of St. Genevieve, on the opposite shore, there stood, a hundred years ago, a fortress, whose ordnance could have absolutely forbidden their ascent!

In 1762 France ceded her territory east of the Mississippi to England. In July 1765 its commandant, St. Ange, retired to St. Louis with its garrison. An attempt to demolish the walls by cannonade from batteaux, is said to have been made by the retreating French, though in vain; and some of the brass and iron ordnance was thrown into the well and the river. Captain Sterling of the Royal Highlanders then took possession, and for nearly ten years maintained the absolute government commenced by the French. In 1772, a portion of the walls having been thrown down by the Mississippi, the place was abandoned, never to be occupied again. In 1783 England ceded the territory to the United States; but its fortress was a ruin. Nevertheless, despite the forest of gigantic trees and the wilderness of tangled undergrowth, wild vines and shrubbery which now hold undisputed possession of the spot, the lines of massive fortification can yet be traced out. Some of the masonry, indeed, seems as solid as it was a century since; although for more than eighty years it has been exposed to the elements, and for more than fifty years served as a quarry of material for all the neighboring villages, and even for distant St. Louis, fifty miles above. Some of the forest-trees which fling their shadows over the ruins of Fort Chartres, are of enormous size. Thirty years ago, in 1822, an oak eighteen inches in diameter is said to have stood in the hall of the commandant's edifice!

In 1765, when the British took possession of Fort Chartres, there was a considerable village in the neighborhood, known as Chartres village or St. Philippe, so called in honor of Philippe Francois Renault, who, in 1719, planted himself on the spot with two hundred miners, in sanguine search of the precious metals. He found nothing more precious, however, than lead at St. Genevieve and copper at Peoria, though the whole region adjacent to the village which he founded is to this day known as "the Renault Tract." In 1765, when English rule began, St. Philippe is said to have boasted not less than forty families, a church dedicated to St. Anne, and served by a Franciscan friar, a water-mill on Barbean's creek, vast herds of cattle in the surrounding meadows, and an extensive, highly-cultivated and richly-productive common-field. But many of the villagers then removed to St. Genevieve, St. Louis, and the other hamlets across the Mississippi, preferring French rule to English, Spain having some years before ceded her possessions west of the Mississippi to France. Three years later, on the 6th of November, 1768, the first court of justice in Illinois was established, "commissions of the peace having been granted by John Wilkins, Esq., Governor and Commandant of the said county." Among the names of these magistrates we find that of Jean Baptiste Barbean, with which name, by the by, we have already met at the cliffs of Prairie du Rocher. The six justices then took and subscribed their oaths of office, as also of allegiance to his Majesty George the Third; as did, also, the sheriff, the Governor and Commandant aforesaid, entering into a recognizance of £500 lawful money of Great Britain for the said sheriff's due performance of his office—all of which may be found more fully set forth in the official archives of Randolph county, in the State of Illinois.

In 1778, Gen. Geo. Rogers Clarke having crossed the Alleghanies, descended the Monongahela and Ohio, struggled through a hundred and thirty miles of wilderness to Kaskaskia and having taken the place by surprise at night, without a blow, mounted his troops on the "Point Ponies," and by a skillful *ruse* took the villages of Fort Chartres and Cahokia from a British force far exceeding his own. Then hurrying off to Vincennes, in a fortnight he had crossed the Wabash in the night, and, by the repetition of the same *ruse*, had caused Gov. Hamilton to surrender Fort St. Vincent, to less than half the force of his own garrison!

But the old hamlet of St. Philippe has long since passed away. Thirty years ago some of its ruined structures marked its site; but even they now are buried beneath the mould of a rank and luxuriant vegetation, while the entire common-field is embraced in a single farm.

Legend and tradition have been busy with old Fort Chartres and the neighboring hamlets; and among these tales of the olden time has not been wanting, of course, that tradition of buried treasure, which ever pertaineth to ancient ruins. The architect of Fort Chartres far exceeded his instructions, so runs the story, in the erection of such an enormous and useless mass of masonry on such a solitary spot; and on its completion, was recalled to France to render an account of his stewardship. Immense sums of gold—nine millions of livres, indeed, had been forwarded to him from New Orleans to pay off his men. But he buried the treasure beneath the foundations of his work, hastened off for France, and in despair of pardon, drowned himself on the passage. And numberless have been the searchings for that same buried gold—year after year—generation after generation—almost century after century—but, as is ever the case with buried gold, all in vain. A western writer has made the tradition the subject of a tale entitled "The Last of the Money Diggers," the scene of which is the ancient fortress and the neighboring village, yet more ancient, of Prairie du Rocher.

THE MISSISSIPPI BELOW ST. ANTHONY'S FALLS.

From the Falls of St. Anthony to Fort Snelling at the mouth of the St. Peter's or more properly Minnesota, a distance of seven or eight miles, the Mississippi pursues its rapid course through a deep ravine overhung by impending cliffs and shaded by shaggy woods. This ravine recalls that below Niagara, and doubtless owes its origin to a like cause. The geological basis of all this region is a thick stratum of shell lime-rock, underlaid by sandstone. As far down as Lake Pepin this characteristic prevails; and the Maiden Rock is equally divided between the two classes. The effects of a stream like the Mississippi, flowing for ages over a surface like this, are obvious. Originally, without doubt, the river had its principal descent at the mouth of its lesser tributary, seven miles below, just as that of the Niagara river was originally, without doubt, at Queenstown. But the recession of the latter stream through the harder rock, of which its cliffs are composed, has been far less rapid than that of the former. Through fissures in its bed of limestone, the waters of the Mississippi reached the crumbling substratum below; and, washing it away, the superincumbent ledge sank in broken masses, or was piled up in Titanic slabs on either side. Above the Falls the stream yet pours over a smooth bed of lime-rock; and the vast mill-dam, more than seven hundred feet in extent, has its base securely bolted to that adamantine floor. So rapid, however, is the dip of the two strata from this point, that, when the stream has worn for itself the same extent of bed above the Falls that it has below, it is evident that a perpendicular descent will no longer exist, and that only rapids will remain. The same fate is predicted for Niagara itself; and when the mighty waters have worn away the rocks, over which they flow from Lake Erie, in the same manner as they have those below on their course to Lake Ontario, the fearful cataract will have disappeared!

It need hardly be said that a scene made up of elements like these, is romantic and

DRAWN AFTER NATURE

For the Proprietor: HERRMANN J. MEYER.

THE MISSISSIPPI

Sunrise below St. Anthony's Falls.

Published for HERRMANN J. MEYER. 164. William-Street. NEWYORK.

sublime; while at the hour which our artist has so well selected to depict it—the hour when the rising sun is chasing from cliff and forest-top the mists of morning, it is eminently lovely. Nothing, indeed, can be conceived more quiet, more placid, more calmly beautiful than this shaded ravine, in the heart of midsummer, beneath the first blush of day. The cliffs, the rocks, the rapids, the woods, the trooping mists, the shifting lights and the heavy shades combine to constitute a scene of indescribable charms. The numerous islets around the cataract, some of them mere masses of rock, and some crowned with shrubs and trees like fresh and green boquets sprinkled by the mists and swayed by the rushing waters, constitute by no means the least attractive feature of the scene.

The action of the river on its bed is strikingly illustrated in the formation of the Fountain Cave, some four or five miles below. Here, entering through a graceful arch some twenty feet high, we find a suite of apartments, four in number, varying in dimensions and extending some hundreds of feet. Through the middle of the cavern in a deeply-worn channel glides the stream, forming several basins and cascades, while far away its murmurings fall on the ear, as it comes dashing in darkness on. The yielding character of the walls is indicated by the numerous names and initials which have been left upon them by the knives of visitors. Just below this natural grotto a small stream comes rushing down the cliffs some sixty or eighty feet in a series of cascades, as snowy as the cliffs themselves; and, still farther down, indeed below St. Paul's, is seen the entrance to a second cave, known as "Carver's Cave," now closed by a fallen mass of the impending cliffs. This cave is said to be spacious, and to contain a lake regarded with much veneration by the Indians. It was discovered by Captain Jonathan Carver, of Canterbury, Connecticut, great grandson of the first Governor of Plymouth, who was with Montgomery at Quebec, and who subsequently explored all this region and gave his adventures to the world. It was at this cave, in 1767, that the Sioux, in consideration of their great regard for the explorer, as he asserts, made him a grant of a vast body of land, extending from St. Anthony's Falls to the mouth of the Chippewa, thence east for a hundred miles, and thence north about a hundred more to the point of starting. This tract embraces the site of St. Paul, and is known as the "Carver Tract." The grant is not deemed valid, however, for several reasons, the chief of which seems to be that it was made in direct violation of the English laws of the period; and it has been repeatedly ignored by Congressional committees. The first claim on the site of St. Paul was made by Gervais, a Canadian. In 1837 this was followed by several others located in the vicinage of Carver's Cave below; but in 1840 the Military Reservation of Fort Snelling was extended so as to embrace ten miles square, going above the Falls and going below the St. Peter's, or more properly the Minnesota, including the village of Mendota at its mouth, and expelling all settlers, whatever their claim. Gervais sold the remnant of his claim in 1843, for some three or four hundred dollars; and, in the summer of 1848, the first sale of Government lands on the present site of St. Paul's at one dollar and twenty-five cents per acre was made.

Settlements on the west side of the Mississippi above St. Paul's, from the mouth of the Minnesota to the Falls of St. Anthony, being precluded by the Military Reservation of Fort Snelling, the only town laid out in the neighborhood is on the eastern side of the river, opposite the cataract, and bearing its name. Not far below is the point in the Rapids which is, probably, destined to become the head of navigation. Indeed, small steamers have already ascended to this point; while above the Falls they have penetrated to Fort Gaines, at the mouth of Kagi-wi-gan, or Crow Wing River, nearly two hundred miles, and with few improvements, will, no doubt, ere long, surmount the series of rapids, half a dozen in number, and ascend a distance of three hundred miles into the heart of the Indian country beyond.

DRAWN AFTER NATURE

For the Proprietor: HERRMANN J.MEYER.

THE STONE WALLS

(UPPER MISSOURI)

Published for HERRMANN J.MEYER. 164. William-Str. NEWYORK.

THE STONE WALLS.

Our engraving represents a view on the right bank of the Missouri, near the Rocky Mountains, about four hundred miles above the mouth of the Yellow Stone, and some forty or fifty miles below that of the Marias river. The line of castellated battlements extending for a long distance on one, and sometimes on both sides of the Missouri, between the Marias and Yellow Stone, has been denominated by the mountain men The Stone Walls. As a generic term for a long line of precipitous cliffs of various and often grotesque forms, and all of the same geological character, it is appropriate enough. But the view before us, though partaking of characteristics common to many others in that wild, mountainous region, is sufficiently unique to deserve a specific name. After counselling with several intelligent gentlemen who are intimately acquainted with the scenery along this part of the Missouri and with this cluster of rocky pinnacles in particular, we have given it the name of the Minarets.

For sublimity, picturesque grandness and wildness, the scenery of the Rocky Mountains is not exceeded in any part of the globe. The Missouri river has three principal forks in these mountains, which have been named Jefferson, Madison, and Gallatin, by Messrs. Lewis and Clark, their first explorers. These unite their waters just above the cataracts, where they rush through a frightful gorge between perpendicular walls. Steep black rocks jut out from the mountains, and rise one thousand feet or more above the foaming river. These mountains vary exceedingly in appearance. Some are bare rocky ridges, and have an aspect of terrific wildness. Others are thinly clad with cedar, pine, fir and other trees; wide plains of a thin, stony and clayey soil, and narrow ravines and gorges are intermingled. The cataracts extend for nearly twenty miles; the river foams and dashes over precipices with a noise like distant thunder. The first cataract measures ninety-eight feet descent; the second, twenty; the third, forty-seven; and the fourth about twenty-six feet.

Below these falls the placid and beautiful river, called by the Canadian French Marias, comes in from the north, and mingles its peaceful waters with the impetuous torrent of the Missouri.

The "Stone Walls" commence a few miles below the embouchure of the river, and continue with intervals, exhibiting every variety of shape and aspect, often sublimely beautiful, then wild and terrific, for many miles. With breaks for the entrance of rivers, and tracts of alluvial bottom land, rocky eminences continue nearly to the Yellow Stone.

In one part they form immense and perpendicular walls of massive rock, divided by seams into huge blocks, and rising upward several hundred feet. Such a view, about one hundred feet in height, is seen on the left in the engraving. Anon they are broken into crags, then they take the form of towers, of baronial castles in ruins, and of lofty spires.

The top of the Minarets, including the base of the mountain on which they rest, is about six hundred feet above the surface of the river. The rock of which these objects and the range of walls are composed is a species of sand stone, by no means uniform in appearance. It is of various colors in different positions, and sometimes in the same cliffs, being represented by intelligent explorers as reddish, yellowish, white and dark brown, or nearly black; some persons represent these rocks as indurated portions of earthy matter. The alternate snows and rains in this region for ages past have washed down the more friable portions, leaving the harder parts to assume the fantastic shapes in which they now appear.

The Rocky mountains proper, whose lofty peaks are first seen on the Missouri, at Marias river, are immense ridges of granite. They are a series of ridges and spurs shooting off in various directions. Some are bare, bleak rocks, destitute of soil or vegetation; others are scantily covered with a few stunted trees and shrubs, while in the defiles and gorges, grass and other vegetation furnish a scanty subsistence for the buffaloes, big-horns, antelopes, and other animals that perchance, for a few weeks in summer, may be found in this inhospitable region. The Minatarees, Black-feet, Cheyennes, Upsarokas or Crows, and a few other ferocious and predatory bands infest this wild mountainous district during the game season.

Further down the mountain slope, in the range of the stone walls and minarets, among the mountain peaks, are tracts of level or gently undulating land of a thin clayey soil, intermixed with pebbles and boulders that may yet furnish support for a sparse population, when the red man has passed away. Those who prefer a pure mountain air, where fevers and other diseases are rarely known, to the rich but less healthy soil below, will make these mountains their abode.

Far off in a southern direction, and near the overland route to Oregon lie the Black Hills, intersected by mountainous belts of sand and limestone. The chain commences near the great bend of the Missouri, and stretches along in a southwestern direction to the south fork of the Nebraska or Platte river. It forms a dividing ridge between the waters of the Missouri and those of the Arkansas. Like the region along the line of the Stone Walls it is composed of sandstone of the same species, and in many places exhibits the forms of castles, towers, towns, church spires and fortresses. The Indians of the plains, and the demi-civilized Rangers of the forests, and mountain Trappers clothe the mountains with superstitious attributes, and fancy they are the abodes of good and evil spirits. The reverberating thunder is the voice of the *Wakon*, and the gleams of lightning are the flashing of his eyes. The hollow moaning winds are the murmurs of unhappy ghosts, and the sweeping storms of hail, and the devastating hurricanes are the tokens from the spirit of evil. On entering the defiles of the mountains, they hang offerings of tobacco and valuable trinkets on the trees, or place them on the rocks to propitiate the favor and avert the anger of these mountain spirits. They watch the clouds as they roll along the mountains, and observe their changing hues, and fancy they can distinguish the good from the evil spirits in their awful visitations.

THE GRAND TOWER.

The great streams of the Western Valley, in their ceaseless flow of ages, have written their annals in most significant characters upon their banks. Roaming onward through vast plains and forests, their mighty floods, rushing from side to side, have scolloped a fringe of Points and Bends in close succession, and with remarkable regularity. And the Point is always opposite to the Bend—the Bottom is always opposite to the Bluff—the soil scooped out by the capricious current from one bank, is always, with that justice which "robs Peter to pay Paul," thrown up in alluvion on the other; while at the mouth of every tributary, however large, however small, always rises an island of proportionate magnitude.

But it is when the everlasting floods encounter "the everlasting hills" in their resistless course, that the most striking results are beheld. Upon the Ohio—upon the Missouri—upon the Mississippi—upon all the Western rivers, these phenomena are more or less observed. Upon the Ohio—below the Narrows where it has ploughed for itself a path through the cliffs, and above its junction with the Mississippi at Cairo—these remarkable characteristics are witnessed in the "Cave-in-Rock," the "Tower Rock," the "Battery Rock," and other similar formations, grotesque or grand, with significant names. Upon the Mississippi the most remarkable of these rocky formations are beheld below St. Louis, commencing near the city, and extending, with little interruption, more than sixty miles on the route to Cairo at the mouth of the Ohio. They are most conspicuous on the Missouri shore, although similar bluffs and cliffs, for more than a hundred miles, bound the great American Bottom, which expands itself on the opposite side.

At the city of Alton, some twenty miles above St. Louis, and near the mouth of the Missouri, terminates a range of eminences called the "Piasa Cliffs." These cliffs are of remarkable formation, some hundreds of feet in altitude, and owe their name to

DRAWN AFTER NATURE

For the Proprietor HERRMANN J. MEYER

GRAND TOWER AND DEVIL'S BAKEOVEN

(MISSISSIPPI RIVER)

Published for HERRMANN J. MEYER 164. William-Street NEW YORK.

an Indian tradition of the Piasa, or "bird that devours men," a representation of which legendary bird with outspread wings is beheld on the embattled façade.

In these cliffs, also, are several caves. At Alton the bluffs begin to recede from the river, leaving an interval of alluvion; and thus commences the celebrated American Bottom, so called because once the limit of American territory on the Western frontier. From Alton, its northern boundary, to Chester at the mouth of the Kaskaskia, its boundary on the south, is a distance of a hundred miles; while its average breadth is about five, embracing a tract of three hundred thousand acres of the most fertile land in the world. In proof of this is the fact that, year after year, for more than a hundred years, in the vicinity of the French villages sprinkled upon its surface, crops of corn at the rate of seventy-five bushels to the acre, have been raised. On one side of this vast meadow rise the heavy bluffs, and on the other along the Mississippi extends a belt of enormous forest trees; while in the space between are beheld farms, lakes, lagunes and island-groves of apples and plums.

It is directly opposite to this remarkable tract, across the river, on the Missouri side, from St. Louis southwardly for a distance of sixty-two miles, that the range of cliffs extends, of which the Grand Tower is the lower terminus. Leaving St. Louis, they first arrest the eye immediately below the United States Arsenal, near the old village of Carondelet, a distance of five miles, and are surmounted by attractive edifices. Twenty miles below comes in the Memiwack, a small and sparkling stream, through an escarpment of castellated cliffs known as the "Cornice Rocks," because of the almost architectural regularity of grooving which they display. The bluffs of Herculanum and Selma crowned with shot-towers next attract the attention. The site of the former place is the mouth of Joachim Creek, which has opened for itself a channel through the rocky façade; and a few miles west of the place rises a remarkable mass of limestone, a hundred feet long and fifty feet high, completely isolated, and completely honey-combed! At the old Spanish town of St. Genevieve ceases this first range of heights, and those which are next beheld, about a mile below, are the remarkable formations which are the subject of our engraving. On every side, as this spot is approached, is beheld undeniable evidence of some fearful convulsion of nature; but whether of a volcanian or neptunian origin—of a volcanic or a diluvial character, or of both united, has given rise to much speculation. Vast masses of rock are said by geologists to dip in every direction, and the whole stratum, for twenty miles around, lies completely broken up. The rock, like nearly all in the Western Valley, is limestone of secondary formation, and abounds with marine and other petrifactions hundreds of feet deep.

The first of the peculiar formations which is passed in descending, consists of two huge masses of rock on the Illinois shore, one of which bears the name of "Devil's Bake Oven." This promontory, which abruptly terminates the bluffs of the American Bottom, commenced at Alton, is about sixty feet high, and from its southern side is scooped out the hemispherical orifice which gives it a name. The huge mass of cliffs in front has evidently been torn from that which now impends. At the base, on the narrow interval of bottom, stands a dwelling surrounded by a small orchard.

Sweeping past the "Bake Oven," we behold a group of cliffs and columns diagonally opposite about a mile distant, and apparently isolated in the midst of the flood. Such however is the fact with but one of them—"The Grand Tower,"—all the others being connected with the shore. The "Tower" is a huge perpendicular mass of lime-rock, about fifty feet high from the ordinary surface of the water, and more than a hundred feet in circuit at the base. On its summit a thin stratum of mould supports a few stunted evergreens; while the turbid torrent boils and rages in a dangerous eddy below. This spot has witnessed several sad catastrophes; one of the latest occurred during the inundation of 1844, when a small boat was dashed against the cliffs and all its inmates were whelmed beneath the waves. On another occasion a bridal party of four persons crossing the river in a skiff were drawn into the whirlpool, and, with a single exception, all perished, and that too within full sight of friends and relatives, who heard in vain their cries for help!

Below the "Bake Oven" and the "Tower" are other singular formations, known as the "Devil's Tea-table," "Backbone," "Anvil," "Pulpit," "Grave," &c.; indicating pretty plainly, as has been said, the divinity most propitiated by western boatmen in these perilous passes. The river pours with fearful force and rapidity through this narrow channel; and before the introduction of steamboats, it was one of the most dangerous points between St. Louis and New Orleans. The ordinary oar or pole was, of course, useless, and the last and only resort was the "cordelle." Landing from their keels or barges at the foot of the rapids, the whole crew applied themselves to the long cord attached to her prow; and drawing, foot by foot, along the shore, they were sometimes whole days in overcoming the obstacle. Sometimes their barque was wrecked upon the rocks, and sometimes they themselves were robbed and even murdered by bands of robbers which haunted the caves and cliffs.

The navigation of this narrow passage, even at the present day, by the splendid steamers of the West, ascending heavily-laden, is not entirely devoid of danger; and all the vast powers of their mighty engines are often requisite, and sometimes almost unavailing, to overcome the tremendous flood. The Mississippi at this point is exceedingly narrow, being less than a mile in width; and with the single exception of a point some six hundred miles above and equally narrow, it is the only one on the whole length of the stream from Fort Snelling to New Orleans, where a rocky shore is presented on either side. The Grand Tower is also, with a single exception, the only island of rock, all the others being composed of alluvial deposite. This exception is found in the celebrated "Mountain which soaks in the water" of the upper Mississippi, several hundred feet high, and more than a mile in circumference at the base. The main channel of the river is here about a mile wide.

With the two exceptions named, no where on the Mississippi is found a rocky shore on both sides. In all other instances if there are bluffs on one side there is inevitable bottom-land on the other. This circumstance has suggested the idea of a bridge to span the stream at both localities. Such a structure is contemplated in the project of a Railroad, connecting the far eastern and far western states of the North; and a company was incorporated by the Legislature of Illinois years ago for the construction of a bridge at the Grand Tower. Nature has furnished her own hills for abutments of such a work, and a base of adamant for the founding of piers; while the mineral and agricultural resources on either side equally exhaustless, and the vicinity of the Iron Mountain and Pilot Knob would seem abundantly to warrant an enterprise so considerable. Nor should the vast water-power, which the Mississippi would afford at this point, be forgotten in the enumeration of its advantages.

Owing to the narrowness of the Mississippi at the Grand Tower, and the obstructions in its channel, it is always the first point at which the river becomes gorged with the floating ice of winter. The landing, however, on both sides is secure, and catastrophes, from this cause, are of unfrequent occurrence; although a score of boats sometimes lie ice-bound for weeks above and below. But a few hours of rain, or a few hours of sunshine will often cause the heaped-up masses to sink; and the passage which at dusk was hermetically sealed, is at dawn miraculously opened. The ice has by magic disappeared, and the fleet of steamers proceeds rejoicing.

The remarkable phenomena at the Grand Tower and in its neighborhood have given rise to much speculation. That the entire region, embracing an area of a hundred square miles, has been the scene of some tremendous convulsion of nature, upheaving from its depths its vast substratum of calcareous rock, geological research has rendered certain. All over this region is scattered a confused accumulation of debris covered with alluvial deposite; while in some places blocks of limestone protrude thirty feet above the surface. As we approach the Grand Tower, this phenomena becomes more astounding. It is plain that the titanic crags which frown upon one side of the narrow strait were once united to those equally titanic which frown upon the other. It is plain, that the rocks of dark limestone on one side of the gulf, imbedding petrifactions, are but a continuation of the same on the other. It is plain, that the deep lines traced on the cliffs on either side, at an altitude of a hundred and thirty feet from the present surface of the river were ploughed by the attrition of rushing waters for hundreds, perhaps thousands of years. It is plain, that a huge parapet of limestone, the base of which may yet be traced, once extended across the Mississippi, from the Tower to its kindred crag, creating a cataract, which would probably compare with even that of Niagara itself. Whether this vast barrier was broken down by some convulsion of nature, or by the continued abrasion of the crushing waters upon the secondary stone, may be a subject of speculation. Of its primitive existence, however, there can be little doubt entertained; while its effects would be obvious. Elevate the waters of the Mississippi a hundred and thirty feet by a parapet at the Grand Tower, and you submerge all the lands lying at a lower altitude, for a hundred miles above. And this is exactly what science and observation teach us had been the fact.

From the Grand Tower to the mouth of the Missouri, on one side, and from the Bake Oven to the Illinois, on the other, stretch two ranges of bluffs, sometimes presenting rounded and graceful knobs, grassy and green, and forest-crowned, and at others exposing a naked escarpment of mural cliffs. The average altitude of these heights is about one hundred and fifty feet; and along their whole course, especially at the Cornice Cliffs already named, are traced the same remarkable groves, at the same remarkable elevation, and with the same remarkable regularity. As you ascend the river, the water-lines become gradually less elevated, obscuring the natural level of standing water, although the parallelism continues.

Thus then, by the mighty parapet at the Grand Tower, was formed a vast lake bounded on either side by bluffs, as far up as the mouths of the Missouri and the Illinois. From the mouth of the former river expands a tract of bottom land, second only to the American Bottom itself, called the Mamelle Prairie, extending up the Mississippi some sixty or seventy miles, and being on an average five or six miles in breadth, bounded by bluffs. Of the alluvial character of this vast tract, there can exist no more doubt than of that of the American Bottom itself. Pebbles, shells, masses of coal, and logs of pine would have been found at a depth of twenty to fifty feet below the surface; and the soil throughout seems a sillicious or angillacious loam, and equally fertile at any depth. That these vast plains were formed by the alluvial dispositions of the annual floods of the river, in the course of ages, is certainly probable; but it is far more probable, connecting these phenomena with the others named, that they once constituted the bed of a lake,—a lake more than a hundred miles long, and some eight or ten miles in average breadth—bounded on the south by the rocky barrier at the Grand Tower, on the east and west by lofty bluffs, while on the north a limit was presented by the gradual and natural elevation of the valley. That centuries—ages have elapsed since this lake was drained, the ancient mounds upon its surface alone would demonstrate; while it is equally plain that the "Mother of Floods," if not the "Father of Floods,"—the Missouri if not the Mississippi—are intent upon resuming their ancient sovereignty. The former stream is annually ploughing into the deep mould of the American Bottom, opposite its *embouchure;* and it has to accomplish but a few hundred yards to pour its waters into the chain of lagunes which will afford it a channel to the bluffs; while the two vast streams united have more than once, during the present century, made the American bottom the bed of a lake for months, as truly as it could ever have been ages ago.

DRAWN AFTER NATURE. For the Proprietor: HERRMANN J. MEYER.

MISSISSIPPI - SCENERY

BETWEEN LAKE PEPIN & St CROIX RIVER.

Published for HERRMANN J. MEYER, 164, William-Street, NEWYORK.

DRAWN AFTER NATURE

For the Proprietor: HERRMANN J. MEYER.

GRAND - SPIRIT - TABLES

(LAKE PEPIN)

Published for HERRMANN J. MEYER 164, William-Street, NEWYORK.

SCENERY BETWEEN LAKE PEPIN AND ST. CROIX RIVER.

THE scenery on the Upper Mississippi between Lake Pepin and the mouth of the St. Croix, though less grand and imposing than that of the region of country above or below, is hardly less lovely and picturesque. The eye does not rest on the same ragged cliffs and rocky walls, indeed, by which it has been impressed either below or above; but the beauty of the woodland and the island scenery is vastly increased. At the very head of Lake Pepin, as your bark emerges from the broad expanse of that beautiful water-sheet, the chain of islands begins with one long and narrow, deeply shaded by vine-clad forests, a dozen miles in extent; others less spacious succeed, from the mere clump of evergreens amid the clear sparkling waters, to an expanse of alluvion ample enough for a farm. Near the upper extremity of this "Twelve Mile Island," on the western shore, is the ancient site of a Sioux encampment, known for many years as Red Wing Village—the name having been derived from that of *Dootah*, or Red Wing, a celebrated chief, who, upon his decease, was succeeded by *Mah-pa-ya-mu-zah*, or Iron Cloud, of later date. At this spot, ever since the earliest explorations of the river, has existed an Indian town; and the conical skin lodges of the Sioux, rising among the leaves and branches, and wreathing them with smoke, lend that air of the picturesque by which savage life is so often invested. The distance from St. Louis is about six hundred and seventy miles. Near the village is an eminence named by the early French explorers *La Grange*, from its resemblance in outline to a barn. It is said to be nearly a mile in extent, and some three or four hundred feet in altitude, with an ancient mound on the summit, as is usual with these "earth o'er looking" heights, from which is viewed the whole expanse of Lake Pepin below, and the Pilot Knob and Fort Snelling, sixty miles distant, above.

The twin mountains of Wapasha and Red Wing—the "Sugar Loaf" and the "Barn"—are by no means the only eminences of interest on the Upper Mississippi, between Lake Pepin and St. Croix, although, as already stated, the face of the country is in this region, for a distance of forty or fifty miles, rather undulating than hilly. Here is beheld a range of remarkable heights characteristic in aspect of the Upper Mississippi, but no where more conspicuous than here. One group of these eminences presented by our artist, is distinguished by the appropriate name of "GRAND SPIRIT TABLES." Rising from masses of tangled forest and undergrowth which fringe their base even to the water's edge, they abruptly slope a few hundred feet, when, suddenly, from the green woodland protrudes the limestone cliff, a naked precipice for some rods in perpendicular height. And there upon the broad table of the rocky summit is spread a green bluff of earth, sprinkled with trees. Graceful as are these singular eminences they are not without grandeur and even sublimity, when with them are associated the legendary traditions of the ancient dwellers in this beautiful region. Nor is it wonderful that these majestic prominences should have been deemed the altars of the Manito—the favored spots on which the Great Spirit was wont to plant his foot when he came down from his celestial home to survey the pleasant land bestowed as a heritage on his red children of the forest. And when the night is still, and moonlight is slumbering mistily on cliff and forest, and the intervening valley is buried in gloom, and the vast river roams steadily onward in its mighty career, can there be an idea more august and solemn than that then the Great Spirit is abroad, and in very presence sits throned on these gigantic heights!

DRAWN AFTER NATURE. For the Proprietor: HERRMANN J. MEYER.

THE EAGLE ROCKS

(MISSISSIPPI-RIVER.)

Published for HERRMANN J. MEYER. 164. William-Street. NEW YORK.

EAGLE ROCKS.

Along the Upper Mississippi river the naked bluffs and rocky cliffs that line the shores, present many picturesque and romantic views. From Lake Pepin, for the distance of fifty miles down, the scenery is grand and beautiful, but varies like a moving panorama as we pass along. The rocks in view are chiefly of the cliff or magnesian limestone, upon a base of sandstone. They belong to that grand division called by modern geologists primary fossiliferous, and to that division termed by some writers the protozoic or silurian system. Frequently the upper portion of the bluff is a naked, perpendicular precipice, extending like a wall along the river, or on the verge of the alluvial bottom-land, or peering up like a regular pyramid. On the western side of the river several of these pyramids appear as if cloven down in their center. About twenty-five miles below Lake Pepin, one of these half pyramids is seen on that side, with grass, herbage, and stunted, dwarfish trees extending to its top. Not far from Wapasha prairie is the range of eminences seen in the engraving, called Eagle Rocks. Among them is a conspicuous elevation called by some the Sugar Loaf, and by others the Twin Mountain. This last name is connected with an Indian legend. Above Lake Pepin there stood a remarkable bluff, with which, in Indian fancy, was associated by joint possession the prosperity of two bands of the Dahcota nation. These were the Ta-lan-ga-ma-ne, or Red-wing, and the *Wa-pa-sha*, Red-Leaf bands. By some breach of diplomatic etiquette, an ardent dispute arose between the leaders of the bands, which resulted in a serious contention for mutual rights in the sacred mountain. Bad birds carried false reports to each chief, and hostile feelings had increased to that extent that the war-dance had been held in each band, and blood was about to flow. The Wa-kan-she-cha, the evil spirit of the Sioux, was bsuily engaged in fanning the flame to bring on a bloody and exterminating war between branches of the same tribe.

The Wapasha party had entered on the war trail with the resolute determination of exterminating the Ta-lan-ga-ma-ne band, who held possession of the sacred hill. This nation believe in and worship Wahkon Tonka, the Father of Life, as the bestower of good; and Wahkon Shecha, the "Master of Evil." They have a third deity, called by a name signifying the Thunderer, who may be properly regarded as an imaginative personification of the explosive electric fluid. The Wapasha party had left the prairie that bears their name, with the intention to surprise and cut off the Red-wings the following night. At this fearful crisis Wahkon Tonka took pity on the deluded bands, and resolved to defeat the wicked machinations of Wahkon Shecha. The aid of the Thunderer was sought. He covered the sky with darkness, and rode on a storm-cloud from his dwelling-place in the far west, sent down torrents of rain and hail, and made the night so fearfully dark that the war party lost their way, and wandered in a contrary direction. Next morning, when the terrific storm had passed over, they found themselves on the Wapasha prairie, in sight of their own village. Amidst the storm and darkness, the "Father of Life" had divided the mountain, and removed one-half to the vicinity of the Eagle Rocks, where it may be seen in the engraving, and left the other half standing above Lake Pepin. Each band now had a share in the sacred hill, and from that period they have been friends.

The country in the rear of these bluffs is undulating, highly picturesque, well watered, with a rich, fertile soil. From the top of the eminences the eye may wander over a broad champaign country, covered with coarse grass, and at the proper season decked with flowers. Groves of trees and copses of shrubbery break the monotony of the vast prairie. The Indian title has recently become extinct to the whole country on the right of the Mississippi, from the upper settlements in the State of Iowa, far above the Falls of St. Anthony, or in the more expressive dialect of the red man, Minverara, or "the water that laughs." Not many years will pass away before the vast region of the Minnesota territory will teem with civilization, and be changed in all its natural features to a productive farming country.

DRAWN AFTER NATURE

For the Proprietor: HERRMANN J. MEYER.

WA-BA-SHA PRAIRIE

Published for HERRMANN J. MEYER, 164 William-Str. NEW YORK.

DRAWN AFTER NATURE

For the Proprietor: HERRMANN J. MEYER.

MOLINE

(JLLINOIS)

Published for HERRMANN J. MEYER. 164 William-Str. NEWYORK.

MOLINE.

Moline, as shown in the engraving, is destined to be a great manufacturing town. It is situated on the arm of the Mississippi that runs between Rock Island and the Illinois Shore, about 200 yards wide, and affording hydraulic power exceeding any other stream in the north western states. The point covered with timber, including the large mill seen on the left, is the upper end of Rock Island. From this point a rock dam has been thrown across the stream and joined to the main shore. This increases the natural descent of the rapids about six feet. The volume of water that passes down this channel can be used for hydraulic purposes to an unlimited extent. As may be seen in the engraving, the river abruptly winds along the shore at the point of observation from whence the view was taken, a short distance below the dam and mills. Steamboats pass up this channel to the mills. The passage for boats is the main channel between Rock Island and the Iowa shore.

The Rock river rapids in the Mississippi commence at Port Byron, a town on the Illinois side, and extend fourteen miles to the lower end of Rock Island. The descent for this distance is twenty-five feet, over a bed of limestone, originally broken by reefs at seven places, which formerly extended across the river. These reefs were partially removed by the United States government in 1837, and the projecting points of rocks, at abrupt turns in the channel, were cut off; but the navigation at low water is still impeded and unsafe. At the moment we are preparing this article, the officers of government are making preparations to recommence the improvement of the channel over these rapids. They are not regular in descent, but greater over the reefs, and less in the channels.

In the immediate vicinity of Rock Island a rather unusual geological phenomenon is presented in its rocky strata. Throughout a large part of the Mississippi Valley above the mouth of the Ohio, the stratified rocks appear in nearly a horizontal position. Their average dip, from observations made by Dr. Locke, is about ten feet in each mile. The strata, generally, belong to the *protozoic*, or silurian system, but are frequently covered with more recently formed diluvial deposits. The *lower secondary*, or carboniferous rocks of this system are found at a lower depth. These two formations comprehend various subdivisions. The coal measures, which extend over a large portion of middle and southern Illinois, run out about twenty-three miles up Rock river. The blue, or pentrimital lime-stone, which in the valley of the Ohio is from eight hundred to one thousand feet thick, shrivels down to a thin substratum and becomes exhausted in this vicinity. The formation in which saline springs are found, and which exist so extensively in Southern Illinois and the middle section of Missouri also terminates here. The cliff limestone, as it is called by Dr. Owen, found but sparingly further south, begins to be developed along the upper rapids, soon swells to an enormous thickness, and becomes the most bulky member of the primary fossiliferous group. It attains the thickness of 550 feet along the river above Prairie du Chien, and seems to engross nearly the whole protozoic system. As we proceed northward, the geological strata appears to rise, until we arrive at a locality a little below the Mountain Island, where in the language of geologists is the *principal axis* of the Upper Mississippi. At that point the lower strata attains its greatest elevation, and declines northward towards the Falls of St. Anthony.

In the immediate vicinity of Rock Island city and Moline, bituminous coal abounds in exhaustless quantities. It is excavated from the bluffs, and as this is near the northern boundary of the great coal basin, the country above must receive its supplies from this point.

The first improvement made on the site of Moline was by Mr. David B. Sears and several associates in 1841, by commencing the dam across the arm of the river, and erecting a mill the following year. In the spring of 1843, the town plot was laid off, and the name Moline (from the French word *moulin*) given to the place. Its progress for several years, was slow, all business in this region being depressed.

Since 1845, its prosperity has advanced in proportion to that of the country. The town now contains one thousand inhabitants, and the number is increasing rapidly. Its situation for manufacturing purposes is not exceeded in the northwest. Rail-roads are rapidly advancing in this direction, and within a brief period, these outlets to a foreign market will be completed. Four large mills for cutting lumber, two of the first class for manufacturing flour, and one of the most extensive manufactories for ploughs in the State are in operation.

An extensive paper mill, and machines carried by water power for working in wood and iron indicate the rapid growth of this embryo city.

In 1852 there were seven stores for retailing goods, two hotels, an academy and three houses for religious worship; one each for Methodists, Congregationalists, and Lutheran seceders; and a society of Baptists, recently organized.

Moline has a quiet, moral, industrious, and enterprising population. It was projected on principles of temperance;—its foundation was laid and moistened with *cold water;* and it retains a character for sobriety.

The soil in the vicinity is a rich, sandy loam, and well cultivated farms are spread over the prairies, and interspersed among the groves of the interior. From the pinnacles of the bluffs, in the rear, a beautiful and magnificent prospect is enjoyed. On the left is the fertile and lovely valley, along which Rock river winds its devious course, with its skirts and groves of timber, and its vast, undulating prairies.

Rock Island lies at your feet, and the bluffs and highlands of Iowa mark the outline of the distant horizon in the west. Turning to the right, the Mississippi, the "great river" of the aborigines, descends in whirl-pools and eddies along the rapids, and dashes against the projecting rocks. Steam-boats are to be seen as they pass up or down the torturous channel, or disappear behind timbered islands and headlands. The roaring of the water as it pours over the dam, the clatter of machinery at Moline, and the low, distant hum of business in the cities of Rock Island and Davenport are indications of their future advancement. These places must become a point of concentration of business and trade, beyond any other on the Upper Mississippi.

CAP À L'AIL.

To the early explorers of the Upper Mississippi,—to the followers of La Salle, Hennepin, Marquette and the Canadian voyagers, their immediate descendants,—is owing the fact, that to nearly every spot characterized for novelty or beauty in the entire extent of the stream, from St. Louis to St. Paul's, there still attach, after a century's lapse, significant names of French derivation. These appellations were always descriptive of the scenes and localities to which they were affixed. Thus, for example, we have the name *La Grange* applied to an eminence near the head of Lake Pepin, because of fancied resemblance to the roof of a *barn;* and that of *La Montagne qui trempe à l'eau,* to a lofty height near the foot of the Lake bathed on all sides by the river which was supposed to *soak* in the water, and which, agreeably to Indian tradition, *sinks* a little in the water, on a certain day of every year. These names bestowed by the early French voyagers, though by no means so sonorous, so poetic, or so significant as those bestowed by the bell-toned idiom of the aboriginal dwellers in this beautiful land, are yet, it must be confessed, far more so than the common place appellations, or the unmeaning Greek and Gothic affixes—the Palmyras, and the Hannibals of the Anglo-Saxon race.

The spot which our artist has so successfully essayed to present on the opposite page, is not only peculiarly rich in tradition, association and scenic charms, but is, also, rich in the number and significance of the French appellations with which it has been graced. It seems, indeed, to have had peculiar attractions both for the voyager and the savage. Nor is it very strange that the fancy of the former should have suggested as a name for the strangely shaped he'ght here given us, the descriptive soubriquet of the *Cap à l'ail,* or the Wing Hill, from the supposed resemblance of its outline to the *wing* of a bird. Its shape, as will be seen, has been as correctly as it has been geometrically described, as "a cone cut from apex to base by a vertical plane."

DRAWN AFTER NATURE

For the Proprietor: HERRMANN J. MEYER.

CAP À L'AIL

(MISSISSIPPI RIVER)

Published for HERRMANN J. MEYER. 164. William-Str. NEW YORK.

But Wing Hill is not the only name by which this singular eminence has been known. It has been called *Cap à garlic,* because of the abundance of wild onions found in the valley below; and *Cap à lingue,* because of the abundance of fish caught in the vicinity; and in the Sioux tongue *Ki-ah-ka-mu-rah,* or Iron Hill, because of the large quantities of that metal found near. At the base of this hill of the many names —as many almost as those of a Spanish grandee at his christening—flows a *slough* of the Mississippi, on the south side of which rises another height, which has been honored almost as much, one of its names being *La Colline du mal,* and another *Le Cap des Puants.* The latter name is said to have owed its origin to the fact, that in the valley at its foot a band of the Puants, the French name for the Winnebagoes, who were about invading the country of the Sioux, were assailed by a band of the latter nation lying in ambush, and massacred to a man. The former title has some connexion, perhaps, with the fact, that, at the base of the hill, is a famous "Medicine Rock," a boulder of granite about the size of a barrel, painted red by the savages, and like all similar geological novelties in this region, held in most sacred regard. A similar boulder, similarly painted and sanctified, is situated at the base of the bluffs below St. Paul's; while some miles below, and just above Prairie du Chien on the western side, rises a cliff called the "Painted Rock," from the fact that, high up on the smooth surface of the limestone, at an altitude apparently inaccessible to savage skill, appear shapeless figures in vermillion hues, which, like similar forms on the Pisa Cliffs near Alton, are objects of the Indian's regard and veneration, as he passes in his canoe.

DAVENPORT, IOWA.

Davenport is a large and flourishing village, the capital of Scott county, in the state of Iowa. It is situated on the west bank of the Mississippi river, at the foot of the Rapids opposite Rock Island, and fronting Rock Island city in the state of Illinois. It was named after Colonel George Davenport, the Indian agent, who was many years associated with John Jacob Astor, Ramsey Crooks and others, in the Fur Trade, and murdered, a few years since, in his dwelling-house upon Rock Island.

Antonine Le Clair, a half-breed, the United States Interpreter for the Sacs and Foxes, in consideration of his faithful services, was authorized by the general government to select, at pleasure, within the territory of Iowa, two tracts of land, each one mile square. His first selection was at the head of the Rock Island Rapids, and his second, fifteen miles below, at the foot of the Rapids; and upon the tract last selected, he laid out a town in 1836–7, and named it after his friend and associate, Colonel George Davenport.

At this period, (1836) the exceeding beauty of the scenery of this interesting locality, was displayed in all its natural attractiveness, and the region round about exhibited few indications of the white man's presence. On the East side of the Mississippi river, were the rich alluvions, wooded hills, the ancient but unoccupied fields and village plat of the Sacs and Foxes, their rude graves and historical associations, with an occasional cabin of the adventurous pioneer and squatter. On the west side were the gracefully ascending and undulating prairies, park-like forests and islands of timber, with scarcely a visible mark or spot made by the hand of civilized man; and in the centre of this unrivalled scenery, was the beautiful Rock Island and old Fort Armstrong, with their traditional and historical recollections.

It was upon this Island that the Indian agent and fur trader, Colonel Davenport,

DRAWN AFTER NATURE

For the Proprietor: HERRMANN J. MEYER.

DAVENPORT

(JOWA)

Published for HERRMANN J. MEYER 164 William-Str. NEW YORK.

resided, and his isolated island-home, surpassed in natural beauty and attractiveness, in-door spaciousness, comfort and luxuries, and out-door tasteful embellishments and productiveness, the far-famed residence of Blannerhasset, as described by the fascinating eloquence of WIRT.

This beautifully diversified, natural scenery, is now materially changed. The populous and flourishing village of DAVENPORT, attracts visitation and permanent settlement, by its beauty of location, its tasteful construction, its healthful climate, the fruitfulness of the surrounding country, and its facilities for internal trade and commerce. Rock Island city has become a large, bustling and prosperous town, with its steamboat landings and railroad depots, and the beautiful Rock Island is soon to become the central pier of a magnificent Railroad Bridge, which is to span the Father of Rivers. The change is, indeed, material and radical, but the combination of the natural and artistical, presents a Panoramic landscape, so grand and so beautiful that it must become a spot of multitudinous summer resort and enduring admiration.

FORT ARMSTRONG, ROCK ISLAND.

Rock Island, in the Mississippi River, is one of the most beautiful in the whole extent of the Father of Rivers. It is situated in the rapids of that noble stream, about one hundred miles south of Galena, and within the territorial limits of the State of Illinois. The country, immediately round about, is exceedingly fertile and surpassingly attractive—indeed, there is no other inland spot of Earth's surface more lovely, attractive and desirable. Here, the Mississippi and Rock Rivers have clear and rapid currents, flowing over beds of rocks and gravel, and bounded by the most lovely shores. Upon the western side of the Mississippi, are a succession of gradually ascending slopes, terminated by a chain of graceful hills, beautified by thinly scattered forest trees, and islands of timber—in appearance, a boundless park, embellished with exquisite taste; and the eastern side is not less beautiful, with its broad alluvial plains and prairies, wooded hills and pure waters.

In the centre of this attractive natural scenery, and a most prominent feature in it, is Rock Island, upon the southern point of which is Fort Armstrong, uplifted on a parapet of rocks.

At a period, so long anterior, that the memory of man runneth not to the contrary, the numerous and powerful *Minneway* or *Illini* Confederacy, inhabited that extensive and fertile region of country, commencing above Rock River, and extending down the Mississippi to the mouth of the Ohio; thence up the Ohio to the Wabash; thence to Fort Wayne; thence down the Miami of the Lake, and thence north to St. Joseph and Chicago. The Sac and Fox Indians, originally residing upon the waters of the St. Lawrence, fought their way to Green Bay, and there uniting with other tribes, made a descent upon the *Illini* Confederacy, and after years of bloody strife and

DRAWN AFTER NATURE

For the Proprietor: HERRMANN J. MEYER.

FORT ARMSTRONG.

Published for HERRMANN J. MEYER. 164. William-Str. NEW YORK.

barbarous warfare, conquered, subjected, and finally exterminated them, and took possession of their extensive and fruitful territory.

Upon the Rock River, just above its confluence with the Mississippi, and in the immediate vicinity of Rock Island, the united and triumphant Sacs and Foxes, founded and built their Capital City; it contained, at one time, several hundred houses, some of them, one hundred feet long, by forty and fifty feet wide, and was among the largest and most populous Indian villages on this continent. It was at this principal village, in 1767, that the renowned Sac Chief, BLACK HAWK, was born; and it was mainly, his refusal to abandon this ancient and national city, the cherished Home of his childhood, and the graves of his progenitors, that occasioned the bloody, expensive and inglorious "Black Hawk war."

For this Capital City and its surroundings, especially, the Rock Island of the Mississippi—the beauty spot of this attractive locality—the Sacs and Foxes had an abiding affection. For a hundred years it had been their national metropolis. Upon a lovely elevation, overlooking the village, the noble rivers and undulating prairies, were deposited the remains of their fathers; and to this rude and savage, but naturally beautiful cemetery, the living annually repaired, to pay a tribute of respect to the departed—to clear away the grass from the graves, and deposit food for the spirits of deceased friends or relatives; and to Rock Island, in immediate proximity, they daily resorted, to gather fruits and nuts which grew in spontaneous profusion—to catch delicious fish in the Rapids, which lave its shores, and to hold personal communion with a Good Spirit, whose favorite abode, according to their traditional belief, was in a cave in the rocks at the southern extremity of the Island.

In 1804, Governor WILLIAM HENRY HARRISON, in behalf of the United States, made a treaty with the Sac and Fox Indians, obtaining the cession of a large tract of country, east of the Mississippi, including their favorite island and ancient city. For this large cession, they were to be paid, annually, one thousand dollars; and the United States, by the 7th article, covenanted and agreed, "As long as the lands which are now ceded to the United States, remain their property, the Indians belonging to the said tribes, shall enjoy the privilege of living and hunting upon them."

In 1816, twelve years after the making of this treaty, and when the nearest frontier settlements had not approached within hundreds of miles of Rock Island, the United States erected upon its southern extremity the frowning battlement-walls of Fort Armstrong. This military fort was an annoyance to the Sacs and Foxes, impaired their fruit-gathering, and hunting and fishing privileges upon their favorite island, and disturbed and violated the sacred abode of the Good Spirit, and finally so alarmed it, that, outspreading its swan-like wings, it flew away and disappeared forever.

Subsequently, and previous to 1829, the United States made frequent attempts to induce the Indians to abandon their ancient and cherished abiding place, and remove to the west of the Mississippi, but the attachment of Black Hawk and his tribe was enduring, and their determination to remain, unchangeable. A technical violation of the letter and palpable infringement of the spirit of the 7th section of the treaty of 1804, was then resorted to. In the year last-mentioned, (1829) when the nearest frontier eastern settlement was still fifty or sixty miles distant, and when the government lands, around, in other directions, had not been offered at public sale, the United States surveyed and sold a few quarter sections of land at the mouth of Rock river, including this Capital City of the Sacs and Foxes. And although Keokuk and his followers acquiesced and urged Black Hawk to yield, and although the United States threatened his ejection, "dead or alive," still the Old Chief and his Braves, would neither go themselves, nor let their people abandon the home and the graves of their fathers, the sacred abode of the Good Spirit, and the prolific fruit and fishing grounds, upon and around Rock Island.

Then ten companies of United States troops were sent to Fort Armstrong, under General Gaines, and were joined by sixteen hundred mounted Illinois militia, under General Duncan; and with this combined national and State military force, Black Hawk and his handful of Braves, with their wives and children, on the 26th of June, 1831, were driven from their village and cultivated fields, to the west bank of the river.

After this, (1832) commenced the Black Hawk war, characterized by bloody incidents and savage slaughter; the battle of Sycamore creek; the attack upon Fort Buffalo; General Dodge's battle on the Wisconsin; the flight of the Indians to the Mississippi; the slaughter of Braves, women and children, while floating on rafts, down the Wisconsin; the battle of the Bad Axe; the capture of Black Hawk and his Warriors; the arrival of General Scott at Rock Island with additional troops; the ravages of the Asiatic cholera among them,—all resulting in the destruction of four or five hundred Indian men, women, and children, about two hundred citizens of the United States, and a cost to the government of about two millions of dollars. And all this sacrifice of blood and treasure might have been prevented, by the payment to the Indians of six thousand dollars, as a compensation for abandoning their village and corn-fields, and to enable them to buy provisions for the fall and winter.

Black Hawk, his two sons, and the Prophet, were at first confined at Jefferson, Missouri, then at Fortress Monroe, at Old Point Comfort, and afterwards, as hostages and captives, exhibited through many of the principal cities and villages of the Union; visiting theatres and public places, and equally dividing with President Jackson, the popular applause and attention.

Fort Armstrong, was selected as the most appropriate place, for the liberation of Black Hawk and his associates, and there they were taken. Fort Armstrong, that was constructed upon and over the cave wherein the Good Spirit dwelt, that had watched over the Sac village, and protected the hunting grounds. Rock Island, so prolific, in former years, of fruits, nuts, flowers, and delicious fish, which had for half a century, witnessed the captive Chief's power and influence, was now to become the scene of his formal liberation, but reluctant submission to his rival, Keokuk.

A commodious room in the Fort was fitted up for the occasion; Keokuk, and one hundred followers, gaily and gaudily dressed in their savage trappings, entered the room and were seated; then Black Hawk and his associate captives appeared and took their seats, dejected. Major Garland arose and addressed the council, and instead of being interpreted that the President requested, he was made to say, that Black Hawk "must listen to the counsels of Keokuk." Whereupon, the Old Chief, with indignant expression and vehemence of manner, exclaimed, "I am a man—an old man—I will not conform to the counsels of any one. I will act for myself—no one shall govern me. I am old—my hair is grey—I shall soon go to the Great Spirit, when I shall be at rest." Afterwards, when the true interpretation was given, he desired "if his speech had been put upon paper, a line might be drawn over it," and then said, "What I said to our Great Father at Washington, I say again, I will always listen to him—I am done."

Progressive civilization has now reached, extended beyond, and overspread the ancient city of the Sacs and Foxes, and their favorite River-Islet; and Fort Armstrong, its spacious courts and pleasant halls, its elevated towers and frowning parapets are deserted and dismantled. Populous cities and villages cover this inland place, and the shrill whistle of the locomotive reverberates among the undulating hills, where, whilom, the war-whoop of the savage was heard.

ST. LOUIS.

Very few cities are there in the United States, to the character, growth, and history of which, attaches so much of interest, as to those of the City of St. Louis. Her history, indeed, is the history of the Upper Valley of the Mississippi, even as is the history of New Orleans the history of the Lower; while, in past progress, in present character, and in future prospects, each city can alone be deemed a worthy rival of the other.

The first man of European origin, who stood on the spot where now stands the City of St. Louis, was, in all probability, the bold Spaniard, Hernando De Soto, Governor of Cuba, with his nine hundred steel-clad followers, in 1541. But the warrior and his followers passed away; and, a year later, "the discoverer of the Mississippi slept beneath its waters." A whole century then elapsed and nearly the half of another, before the experiment of exploration was repeated, and Jacques Marquette, a missionary monk of Laon, and Sieur Joliet, a trader of Quebec, undertook an expedition, authorized by M. Talon, Intendant of New France; and, on the 17th of June, 1673, emerged into the Mississippi, from the mouth of the Wisconsin. A month later they had passed the mouth of the Missouri, and had encamped, possibly, on the bold bluff and beneath the dense shades of that pleasant spot, twenty miles below, which no human vision could then have revealed as the site of the future emporium. Having continued and completed their explorations, for some months, and many hundreds of miles, the trader, true to his instincts, returned to Quebec for his reward, and received the Island of Anticosti, in the Gulf of St. Lawrence; while the pious monk, an Apostle to the savages, years afterwards, alone with his God, yielded up his blameless life on the lonely shores of Lake Michigan.

Ten years later, in 1682, the Sieur Robert Cavalier de la Salle, a Norman of Rouen,

DRAWN AFTER NATURE

For the Proprietor: HERRMANN J. MEYER.

SAN LOUIS

(MISSISSIPPI)

Published for HERRMANN J. MEYER. 164. William-Str. NEWYORK.

with the Chevalier De Tonti "of the iron-hand," and forty men, and Louis Hennepin of Artois, the Jesuit priest, had explored the vast river from one extremity to the other. The Cavalier had descended to the gulf, and claimed the whole vast valley in the name of France, and called it Louisiana in honor of her king; while the Franciscan Friar, with only two priests and seven boatmen, had ascended the stream to the Falls, and named them in honor of St. Anthony of Padua, his patron Saint.

But the fate of the gallant La Salle proved even more sad than that of his adventurous predecessors. Upon a second expedition, he fell, in the wilds of Texas, by the blows of assassins of his own band. His followers, scattered abroad, founded, in 1684, a village on the site of a favorite abode of the Kaskaskia Indians, and gave it their name; while, five years later, a second village on the old "stamping ground" of another Indian tribe called the Cahokias, was commenced, and was permitted to retain its ancient appellation. Catholic missions by the good Father Gravier were soon established; immigration from Canada and from lower Louisiana soon poured in, and, early in the ensuing century, two hundred miners and artificers at one time, led by Philippe François Renault, "Director General of the mines of Louisiana," arrived in search of gold!

Such was the origin and inception of the first settlement of the Western Valley of Upper Louisiana. Thirty years later, on the 14th of September, 1712, the first government was established by France; and to Sieur Antoine Crozat was delegated power to rule that immense realm in accordance with "the laws, usages and customs of Paris." Five years later, Crozat resigned his privileges and powers to a corporation called "The Western Company," directed by the celebrated John Law, who, upon the explosion of his famous "bubble," and the bankruptcy of thousands of his noble victims, resigned the charter, in 1731, and Louisiana was thenceforth, for thirty years, governed by Lieutenants appointed by the king of France.

Meantime, and as early as 1719, war had broken out between the Spanish colonies in Florida and Mexico and the French colonies in Lower Louisiana; and an expedition of Spaniards came over the Plains from Santa Fè with the purpose of rousing the Osage Indians against their hereditary and inveterate foes, the Missouries, in which conflict the Spaniards were to aid them in the work of extermination, provided similar aid should be rendered the Spaniards against their foes, the French, who were allies of the hated Missouries. But the invaders mistook one tribe of savages for the other; revealed to them all their plans, and only one—a priest, out of the whole band, was spared to bear home the bloody tale. To guard against similar expeditions, Captain Burgmont, with a detachment of troops from Mobile, ascended the Mississippi, and thence the Missouri above the Osage, and erected a block-house on an island, calling it Fort Orleans. Still further, to protect the French colonists against their Spanish and savage foes, a cordon of military posts, designed to connect the lakes with the gulf, was commenced along the banks of the Ohio and Mississippi, among which posts was erected, in 1721, the celebrated Fort de Chartres, on the American Bottom, some twenty miles above Kaskaskia, and nearly twice that distance below Cahokia and the future St. Louis, only the ruins of which are now beheld. By this bold policy, the jealousy of England, whose colonies then stretched along the Atlantic coast, was roused, and the "Old French War"—a war of boundary ensued, at the close of which, in 1762–63, by the peace of Paris, France yielded to England the Canadas and all her possessions east of the Mississippi, save New Orleans, and, by secret articles, all her territory west of the Mississippi to Spain; while Spain, in consideration of the restoration of the Havana, which had been occupied by a British fleet, ceded to England the Floridas. Of the vast territory thus lightly ceded, not to say shamefully, at least by France, England took possession in 1764–65; but no authority was exercised over the opposite shore of the river by Spain until 1768. The only settlement, indeed, at that early day on the western bank of the Mississippi, then known as "Western Illinois," or "Upper Louisiana," was the hamlet of Ste. Genevieve, which, for about ten years, had afforded a mart for the staples of the country—peltry and lead. The authority of France was still exercised by D'Abadie, the Governor General of Louisiana, residing at New Orleans, although, as early as April, 1764, he had been directed to announce the cession of the whole territory to Spain by the secret treaty of 1763.

Thus, by the peace of Paris, signed by England, France, Spain and Portugal early in February, 1763, all the French territory east of the Mississippi, New Orleans only excepted, was ceded to England; and, by an article to remain secret for twelve months, all the French territory west of the Mississippi was ceded to Spain.

Some months prior to this event, in 1762, D'Abadie, the Director General and Civil and Military Commandant of Louisiana under the French rule, had granted to Pierre Ligueste Laclede and Antoine Maxan and Company, the exclusive privilege of trading with the Indian tribes on the Missouri and west of the Upper Mississippi, under the name of the "Fur Company of Louisiana." The region inhabited by these savages was, it is true, only a waste and howling wilderness; but the same spirit of daring enterprise then existed which fired the bosoms of the subsequent explorers of the Western Valley, or of those pilgrims of Plymouth, or cavaliers of Jamestown, who had already settled the bleak shores of the Atlantic. The purpose of the company was to found permanent posts for carrying on the lucrative trade in furs and peltry, and also for the mining of lead, and, perchance, of the more precious metals. For the glowing visions of gold which had dazzled the imaginations of the followers of De Soto and La Salle, more than a century before, had not yet entirely faded.

Barges were provided and provisioned and laden with bright cloths, beads, blankets, hatchets, and other articles attractive to the savage eye and taste; and, on the 3d. day August, 1763, the expedition started from New Orleans. To Laclede had been committed the conduct of the enterprise. He was a man of about forty, possessed of great energy and ambition, courteous in manners, intelligent, brave, and indomitably persevering. It is said that he never married, though his name was intimately associated for many years with that of a lady of New Orleans, to whom he was thought to have been tenderly attached. It was under the auspices of D'Abadie, the French Governor, that the expedition started; and it may be remarked, that both its conductor and his associates were in entire ignorance, that, by the treaties of the previous February, the patent under which they acted was null and of no effect, and that to Spain alone belonged jurisdiction over the region for which they were destined.

It was exactly three months to a day—the 3d. day of November—from the time that the barges left New Orleans, before they had accomplished their slow and tedious passage to Ste. Genevieve, a distance of nearly twelve hundred miles; and little could it have been dreamed, that, within the period of a single century, the same voyage would, by the aid of a then almost unknown power, be accomplished within nearly the same number of days as then demanded months. The slow and toilsome navigation of heavily-laden barges against the mighty current of the Mississippi, by means of the pole, the oar, the *cordelle*, and the sail swelled by the occasional breeze, may be better imagined than described.

Ste. Genevieve, as already stated, was then the only settlement on the west shore of the Mississippi. It had been founded in the year 1755, and consisted of a few cabins constructed of logs, standing on a low bottom, since swept off by the river, the dimensions of which cabins may be inferred from the fact, that none were of sufficient capacity to contain the freight of the barges. Ste. Genevieve, however, had been destined to become the principal trading-post of the newly-chartered company; but the keen eye and sound judgment of Laclede at once decided that it was not an appropriate spot for his enterprise. Crossing the river, therefore, to Fort de Chartres, a few miles above, in "the Illinois," and, by permission of the Commandant, Noyon de Villiers, having deposited the contents of his barges in the extensive storehouses of the fortress, he started, with a few followers, in a single boat, to explore the country on the opposite shore as high as the mouth of the Missouri. Among his associates, it may be observed, was a bold, bright boy of thirteen, by the name of Auguste Chouteau. Having reached the Missouri without deciding upon a suitable point for their enterprise, the explorers slowly descended the stream, surveying as they came, until at length, some eighteen or twenty miles below, they reached a spot which at once arrested their attention. From the margin of the water rose a mass of limestone, some eighty feet high, on which, as a foundation, swept off an undulating plain, miles in extent, emerald with vegetation, and free from trees or shrubs, save at one spot, where it descended to the water, where stood a heavy and beautiful grove. It was on this spot that Laclede now landed—a spot where once stood the Old Market-House and City Hall, and on which, within a few years has been erected an extensive block of stores; and here it was, that he resolved to pitch his tent. The site was evidently designated by nature as a dwelling for man; and the numerous groups of mounds by which it was occupied, as well as those so celebrated within a few miles on the opposite shore, proved it to have been a favorite resort for the primitive dwellers of the land. The bold rampart of limestone protected it from the encroachments of the stream; while the river itself, though then deeper, probably, than it now is, was, also, much narrower—so narrow, indeed, that it could be "conversed across with ease." On the broad flat rock on which Laclede landed, it is stated, was beheld the imprint of a human foot, advancing from the water's edge to the plain above, and, seemingly, "marshalling the way which he should go." Were this even so, or, guided by other omens, such as the voice of oracles, or the flight of birds, or the phenomena presented by the entrails of sacrificed beasts, had the spot for the future metropolis been selected, the favorable prognostications would not have been falsified by the result. Having landed, Laclede took possession of the spot, by felling a few trees, and *blazing* others, and named the future town St. Louis, in honor of his sovereign. His followers wished, subsequently, to bestow on the place, the name of its founder, but they failed to obtain his consent.

The winter had now set in with considerable severity, and, to avoid being closed up by the ice, which in great quantities was flowing past, the adventurers entered their boat and descended to the Fort. Their descriptions of the advantages of the site selected for the post are said to have been most glowing, and Laclede was sanguine and enthusiastic in his anticipations respecting his future town. The winter was past in preparations for the new settlement, and in participation of the hospitalities and festivities for which Fort de Chartres and its neighboring villages of Cahokia, Kaskaskia, St. Philippe, and Prairie du Rocher, were always noted.

In a few weeks the navigation opened, and, about the middle of January, Laclede sent a large barge up to St. Louis, manned by thirty men, to prepare for the reception of the stores. A few weeks later, accompanied by the residue of his followers from New Orleans, and several others from Ste. Genevieve and Fort Chartres, and by his young friend, Auguste Chouteau, Laclede himself ascended the river, and, on the 15th of February, 1764, landed on the spot where he had previously taken possession. Trees were now felled, storehouses and cabins were constructed of logs, the outlines of a town were traced out, and the place was formally named in honor of Louis XV., who, by Laclede, in ignorance of the secret treaty, was still deemed the sovereign of the soil.

In April, Laclede visited the Fort, and returned with new colonists from the neighboring villages, whom he furnished with supplies; and, in July, bringing up his goods and stores, together with several families of Cahokia, which he had induced to accompany him as he passed the place, the settlement was fairly commenced, and St. Louis commenced her march to empire. Laclede, subsequently, visited New Orleans, and, in

1778, on his return from that city to St. Louis, near the mouth of the Arkansas, died. On the lonely shore, beneath the aged forests, in a rude coffin, he lay down to his last rest, near the spot where reposed the remains of the first explorer of the Mississippi. But the fate of De Soto, and Marquette, and La Salle, seemed to follow, also, the founder of St. Louis. The exact spot of the burial of each, is unknown. Fifty years later, in the month of February, 1829—sixty-four years from the founding of the city—at an advanced age, at the Post of Arkansas, Col. Auguste Chouteau—he who, as a boy of thirteen, had witnessed the first landing on the site of the future emporium, followed his distinguished friend to the other world. A constant resident, he had beheld the spot emerge from wilderness, and had become one of its wealthiest and most respected citizens.

The growth of St. Louis, during the early years of its existence, was comparatively rapid, and was advanced by the concurrence of several favorable events. One of these was the evacuation of Fort de Chartres by the French. In the spring of 1765, just a year after the founding of the City of Laclede, Captain Stirling, of the British Highlanders, arrived at the fort with a body of troops from Detroit, bearing a proclamation from General Thomas Gage, dated at his head quarters, New York, the 30th of December preceding, by authority of which, in accordance with the treaty of Paris of the 10th of February, 1763, two years before, he demanded possession of the "Country of the Illinois." The proclamation announced to the inhabitants the liberty of the Catholic religion, as already granted to those of Canada; also the privilege of retiring from the country with all their goods, or continuing, at their option, to reside at their old houses, urging upon them "to conduct themselves like good and faithful subjects," thereby saving themselves "the scourge of a bloody war, and all the evils which the march of an enemy into their country would draw after it." The French commandant, Louis St. Angé de Belle Rive, at once surrendered the fortress, together with the villages of Kaskaskia, Cahokia, St. Philippe, and Prairie du Rocher, and, indeed, the whole territory of the Illinois eastward to the Ohio. Some months later, on the 17th of July, St. Angé, with his whole garrison, numbering, however, only one-and-twenty men, accompanied by many of the inhabitants of the neighboring villages, left Fort Chartres and proceeded to St. Louis. Many of the villagers, to whom British laws and manners had already become irksome, crossed the river about the same time to Ste. Genevieve; and the whole French population of "the Illinois," from the Mississippi to the Wabash, was estimated at about five thousand souls, including some five hundred negro slaves.

St. Angé, on his arrival at St. Louis, at once assumed the government of Upper Louisiana. The inhabitants readily acquiesced; and they would, probably, have done the same had they been aware that he had not, nor could have, any adequate authority for this assumption,—had they been aware, that D'Abadie, the Director General, was dead, and that Aubry had succeeded to his office at New Orleans; or, more than all, had they known that they were no longer in any wise amenable to French rule, but, for more than two years, had been, and then of right were, the subjects of Spain. One of the first official acts of St. Angé was to give to the French Colonists right of property to those lands of which Laclede had given them only right of possession; and the grants and concessions recorded in his Land Book, or *Livre Terrien*, form the only basis of title to the most valuable portions of the present city of St. Louis. These grants were, of course, void and valueless *ab initio*, and have so been decided by the highest legal authority in Missouri. French power had ceased by the treaty of 1763, and St. Angé had no power from Spain to grant land, or to do anything else. It may be remarked, however, that all these grants and concessions were recognized and confirmed by the lawful authorities of Spain some years later, on the 23d of May, 1772, which period is the earliest from which Missouri land titles take their date. Indeed, until the year 1766, and after the arrival of St. Angé at St. Louis, no grants of real estate had been made, and no one pretended to be a land-holder, or land owner in fee simple. The whole territory had originally been possessed by the great nation of Illini Indians; but they had quietly acquiesced in their ejectment by the French, and, as was ever the fact, the two races lived on together in the utmost harmony and good neighborhood.

As early as October, 1763, D'Abadie, the French Governor at New Orleans, had been notified of the cession of Western Louisiana to Spain by the treaty of the preceding February, and had been instructed to surrender the province into the hands of the Spanish agents duly empowered to receive it. But such was the dissatisfaction manifested by the inhabitants of New Orleans at this transfer, that no attempt at taking possession was made for nearly two years. Meantime, early in 1765, Milhet, a merchant of New Orleans, was sent as an envoy by the citizens to the French king to deprecate the transfer; but the mission, though twice undertaken, proved bootless, and, in the autumn of 1767, Don Antonio D'Ulloa with two companies of Spanish infantry arrived to take formal possession. Such, however, was the opposition by which he was met, that he deferred his demand for the province, and in October, 1768, was driven from the shores of Louisiana. Delegates were again despatched to Paris, but on the 18th of August, 1769, Don Alejandro O'Reilly, with a strong armament and some four or five thousand troops anchored before the city, and formally took possession in name of his sovereign, Charles III. The population of Louisiana was at that time about twelve thousand in number, of which nearly one-half were negro slaves. The population of New Orleans was about three thousand. A lucrative trade in peltry and lead was carried on with the Illinois, or Upper Louisiana, and the export of deer-skins alone was estimated at the value of $80,000, and of all other articles at nearly $200,000 more. O'Reilly administered the government with extreme severity, having executed six of those most active in opposition to D'Ulloa and sent two others to Havana in chains. A year later he was himself recalled to Spain in disgrace.

Upper Louisiana had, however, been more easily reduced than the Lower. In the spring of 1768, D'Ulloa had dispatched Don Rious, one of his lieutenants, with a body of troops in barges up the Mississippi to St. Louis to take possession. There was no resistance. The inhabitants quietly acquiesced, although St. Angé continued to exercise his assumed authority for more than a year subsequently, and until the opening of 1770. On the 29th of November of that year arrived at St. Louis Don Pedro Piernas, deputed by O'Reilly to be Lieutenant Governor and Civil and Military Commandant of Upper Louisiana, though he did not enter on the administration of government until the month of February ensuing.

But, if the inhabitants of Upper Louisiana did not manifest the same repugnance to Spanish rule as their French brethren of the Lower province, neither had they cause. The new government was hardly less paternal than the old, and so attached to it had the simple villagers become thirty years later, that the retrocession to France was regarded with regret. Attracted by this mild dispensation as well as by the fertility of the soil, the salubrity of the climate, and the lucrative traffic in peltry and lead, immigration now set steadily in from the Canadas where the British yoke had begun to be irksome, and from New Orleans where that of O'Reilly was intolerable; and other settlements were rapidly planted in the neighborhood of St. Louis. Among these was *Les Petites Cotes*,—"The Little Hills," subsequently St. Andrews, now St. Charles, founded by Blanchette Chasseur, in 1679; *Florissant*, subsequently St. Ferdinand in honor of the King of Spain, but now Florissant once more, founded in 1776, the year of the declaration of American independence, by Beaurosier Dunégant; and *Vide Poche*, because of its emptiness of pocket, subsequently Louisbourg, and now Carondelet, in honor of Don Francisco Louis Hector, Baron de Carondelet, Governor and Intendant of Louisiana in 1792, founded by Delor de Tregette in 1767. This little village has claimed priority of settlement even to St. Louis itself. As early as 1765, Baptiste Pugol Catalan, a native of Catalonia, a border province of Spain, whence his surname, is said to have pitched here his tent, and to have given to the beautiful plain on which it stands the name of Prairie Catalan, a name it long retained in ancient deeds.

In 1775, Piernas was succeeded by Don Francisco Cruzat as Governor of Upper Louisiana, and he, in 1778, by Don Fernando de Leyba.

Meantime, British rule on the eastern shore of the Mississippi was by no means so popular with the French villagers as was that of Spain on the western. Captain Stirling, who, early in the spring of 1765, had taken possession of Fort de Chartres died the ensuing summer, thus verifying the declaration made to him on assuming command, that the spot was "fatal to strangers;" and the post being left without a commandant, the amiable St. Angé returned from St. Louis and resumed his functions, until the arrival of Major Frazer from Fort Pitt. The following spring the new commandant was succeeded by Col. Reed, equally odious as his predecessors, who, in the Autumn of

1768, was superseded by Lt. Col. Wilkins. Alienated by the oppressive despotism of British rule, many of the French crossed the river to their countrymen at St. Genevieve, St. Louis, and the other villages named which had now begun to spring up.

In the month of April, 1769, the celebrated Pontiac, war-chief of the Ottawas, visited St. Angé, an old acquaintance, then acting commandant at St. Louis, and passed some days at the Fort, and at the Government House, and at the old stone mansion of Pierre Chouteau. An Indian feast taking place at Cahokia during this visit, Pontiac crossed the river with his followers to attend it, though strongly dissuaded by St. Angé. A joyous carousal ensued; and, while the great chieftain, in a drunken delirium, was singing his medicine songs in a neighboring grove, an Indian of the Kaskaskia tribe, bribed by an English trader named Williamson, with a cask of whiskey, stole behind him, and sank his tomahawk up to the head into his brain. The deed was terrible, and terribly was it avenged in the utter extermination of the Illini nation to which the assassin belonged. The body of the murdered chieftain was begged by his friend, St. Angé, and interred with military honors near the Fort of St. Louis. This fortification, called the Bastim, was of stone, an irregular square in outline, and situated at the present intersection of Broadway and Cherry street. Below, on the river-bank, stood a stone tower called the Half Moon, and between the two was an outpost to defend the approaches, also of stone.

Prior to 1778, Detroit was the head-quarters of the western posts and was connected by a *trace* with Fort Sackville, or Post St. Vincent, now Vincennes, on the Wabash, and with the other posts on the Mississippi: and, prior to 1772, Fort de Chartres was the head-quarters of "the Illinois," after which it was superseded by Fort Gage, on the east bank of the Kaskaskia, opposite the old town. There was, also, a small Fort at Cahokia, on the bank of the Mississippi, some six or eight miles below St. Louis.

Meantime the war of the revolution had broken out in the Atlantic States; and, in 1775–76, a plot contrived by Lord Dunmore, the Royal Governor of Virginia, for the extermination of the dwellers on the frontiers, in concert with the commandants of Detroit and Fort Gage, through the instrumentality of the savages, having been detected by the arrest of one of his agents, Col. George Rodgers Clarke was permitted by Patrick Henry, Governor of Virginia, to undertake a secret expedition for the reduction of the British posts on the Wabash and the Mississippi; and, on the night of the 4th of July, 1778, after having encountered privations and perils innumerable and indescribable in his weary way through the wilderness, with less than four hundred men he took possession of Fort Gage and the town of Kaskaskia without striking a blow. So complete was the surprise, that the commandant of the Fort, the Lt. Governor Rocheblave was arrested while sleeping in his bed by Simon Kenton, captain of one of the corps. On the evening of the same day, Captain Bowman was sent off to surprise Fort Chartres and the town and Fort of Cahokia, in which undertaking he was entirely successful.

Kaskaskia is said to have embraced at that time about a hundred families, Cahokia about fifty, and the smaller villages of Prairie du Rocher, Prairie du Pont and St. Philippe about a dozen each. The French villagers, who had hated the arbitrary rule of the English, recognized with joy the authority of Virginia, upon learning that she was at war with the hereditary foe of their fatherland; and a few days later the inhabitants of Vincennes, under the influence of Father Gibault, parish priest of Kaskaskia, threw off allegiance to England, and declared themselves citizens of the United States. Fort Sackville was soon after captured, and the ensuing October "the Illinois" was formerly declared a County of Virginia, and Col. John Todd was appointed civil commandant. The post of Vincennes was subsequently re-captured by Col. Hamilton of Detroit, and captured again by Gov. Clarke, after which no attempts were made by the British to regain the posts on the Wabash, or on the Mississippi, and the whole country, under the name of the "County of Illinois," remained under the jurisdiction of Virginia until the close of the war, when, by the treaty of September 3, 1783, England relinquished to the United States the whole of her territory east of the great river.

But, while these stirring events had been witnessed on the eastern side of the Mississippi, the inhabitants of St. Louis, on the opposite shore, had not remained entirely undisturbed. Spain, as well as France, had sympathized with the revolted colonies of Great Britain; and, in the spring of 1779, the latter power was at open war with the two former. A year later, the British commandant at Mackinaw planned an expedition against the Spanish settlement of St. Louis, which had well nigh proved successful. Rumor of this purpose having reached the town in the fall of 1779, preparations were at once adopted for its defence. A stockade wall, constructed of a double row of upright posts planted in the ground and filled in with earth, was described in a semi-circle around the village, commencing at a small fort on the river bank at the upper suburbs, and, having swept over the brow of the hill, terminating with a similar fortification at the extremity below. In this stockade there were three gates giving egress to the public "commons," and at each gate stood a heavy cannon, constantly charged. But autumn and winter passed away, and the spring came, and the threatened attack not having been made, the Spanish commandant, De Leyba, succeeded in inducing the belief, that none had ever been designed. So intent was this officer to lull the villagers into complete security, that he ordered an old man named Quenelle, who, one day, early in May, had reported that he had seen Indians on the opposite side of the river where he had been to fish in Cahokia Creek, to be at once imprisoned for needlessly disturbing the peace. Meantime, from the south-western shores of Lake Michigan, where now stands the City of Chicago, had proceeded a host of some fourteen hundred savages, which had secretly and silently assembled—Chippewas, Sioux, Sacs, Menomonees and Winnebagoes—led by a hundred and forty British troops of the regular army, and guided by Canadian French; and, marching down over the prairies, along the identical route now pursued by the Chicago and Mississippi Railroad, had encamped within a few miles of the unsuspecting and devoted city on the opposite shore, and lay quietly in ambush, awaiting the day destined for the attack, the 26th of May. On the previous day, it is said, fell, on that year, the Catholic feast of *Corpus Christi;* and, had the attack then been made, the massacre would inevitably have been exterminating, for the whole village had poured itself out through the gates upon the open prairie to gather strawberries, which were in plentiful profusion. Next morning the enemy crossed the river, and at once advanced on the place. Some twenty of the villagers of those who had gone out to work in the common fields, were slain before they could reach the gates, and their remains were subsequently found horribly mangled. The number of male citizens in the place, at this time, is said not to have exceeded one hundred and fifty. Some weeks before, Don Silvio Francisco Cartabona, a Spanish officer, had brought from Ste. Genevieve, a company of militia, numbering sixty men, for the protection of the place, in case of an attack; but no sooner had the attack commenced, than Cartabona and his men hid themselves away in a garret, and were seen no more until the danger was over! But the French villagers were resolute in their purpose of defençe, hopeless as it might seem through this defection. Sending off the women, children and old men, for safety, to the stone mansion of Auguste Chouteau, erected near the spot of the first landing, as early as 1764, and which continued to stand for more than sixty years later,—a squad of fifteen men was stationed at each of the gates; and so warmly did they receive the advancing hosts with showers of grape from the three pieces of artillery, that the foe was glad to beat a rapid retreat. At this juncture, it is related, that the Governor, De Leyba, for the first time made his appearance, "rolled in a wheelbarrow" to the scene of strife; when, to the amazement of the brave villagers, he ordered the guns to be spiked, and the defence at once to cease: and, not being immediately obeyed, he discharged a cannon at the defenders themselves, from the effects of which they narrowly escaped destruction! The conduct of this man can be accounted for only on the supposition that he had been bribed to treason, by that famous weapon of England at the time—"British Gold." Not only had he sedulously suppressed all apprehensions of attack, and imprisoned those who attempted to give warning, but he had crippled the means of defence by selling all the ammunition in the town, as he had supposed, a few days before to traders. But he was deceived. There still remained eight casks in a private cellar, which were, of course, seized on the first attack. An account of De Leyba's conduct having been transmitted to the brave Don Bernard de Galvez, then Governor-General of Louisiana, at New Orleans, the traitor was promptly removed, and Don Francisco Cruzat, the former Intendant, was appointed to his place. But, overwhelmed by his ignominy, De Leyba had already succumbed to a more mighty avenger, and, on the 28th day of June, just one month after the attack, he was entombed in the old village church, "immediately in front of the right hand balustrade, having received all the sacraments of our mother the holy church," as is set forth duly and at length by the certificate in the ancient Church Register yet existing, entered by Father Bernard, "a Capuchin priest and apostolic missionary curate of St. Louis, Country of Illinois, Province of Louisiana, Bishopric of Cuba."

On the decease of De Leyba, the functions of Goverment were assumed by Cartabona, until the arrival of Cruzat the ensuing year. And thus terminated an attack, the failure of which, considering the multitude of the assailants, the inadequacy of the defence, and the treason or the cowardice of the Governor of the town, may be viewed as little less than miraculous. And as such by the early villagers was it deemed; and ever since, "The Year of the Great Blow"—*L'Année du Grand Coup*—has marked an era in the chronicles of the place.

The sudden departure of the savage hosts, surprised the citizens of St. Louis scarcely less than did their sudden appearance. It has been attributed to various causes. The unlooked-for and resolute resistance of the French—the unexpected presence of walls and fortifications—the effects and the noise of the artillery to which the savages were unaccustomed, are some of the causes to which has been attributed this hasty retreat. The destruction of St. Louis alone seemed designed. The neighboring villages were entirely unvisited, and the numerous herds of cattle and troops of ponies on the commons were entirely untouched. By some writers, the suddenness of this retreat is attributed to the advance of Col. Clark with five hundred Americans from Kaskaskia. On seeing this, the savages, reproaching their British leaders with duplicity, in having assured them they were to encounter only Spaniards, while they had led them, not only against their friends the French, but, worse than that, against the "Long-Knives" of the dreaded Clark,—deserted their colors and returned to the villages on the Lakes. And all this may have been true. It is very certain that Col. Clark, who then commanded at Kaskaskia, having been apprised of the contemplated attack, offered De Leyba his aid; but it is equally certain it was declined. Subsequently the citizens doubting the courage, ability or fidelity of their commandant, may have sent to Clark for the proffered aid. With five hundred men he is said to have marched from Kaskaskia to the bank of the Mississippi, a few miles below St. Louis, and to have there encamped for observation; when, the attack having been made, he crossed the river and put the assailants to flight. It is scarcely probable, however, as has been stated, that "the siege continued a whole week, and that repeated attacks and skirmishes took place," while it is still less so, that "large droves of horses and cattle were driven off"—that "sixty citizens were slain and fifty others taken prisoners, the timely arrival of Col. Clark alone rescuing them from captivity." However this may be, there can be no doubt, that the early French villagers of St. Louis contributed their mite in this affair, to the achievement of the independence of that Union, to which they were so soon to become attached.

The danger to which the rising capital had been exposed by this unexpected attack and its unprotected condition, induced the new Governor, Cruzat, shortly after his arrival from New Orleans, to commence a system of fortifications, of structure so solid as to have endured more than half a century. These fortifications, in addition to the Bastion and Half Moon, already mentioned, consisted of half a dozen square or circular forts of stone, about forty feet in diameter and twenty in height, linked together by a strong and high stockade of cedar posts, and a parapet of stone with loop-holes for musketry. The towers or forts were all supplied with artillery and munitions, and were always manned by soldiers. One of these forts, which stood at the present intersection of Walnut and Fourth streets, served, subsequently, not only as a fort, but, also, as a court-house and a prison. To it, likewise, was attached a cemetery.

Nothing again occurred at St. Louis of sufficient importance to be dated from as an epoch, until the month of April, 1785, when the Mississippi at its spring flood rose thirty feet above the highest mark before known, sweeping off half the houses in Kaskaskia, and so covering the American Bottom with water, that the bluffs and the French villages were visited by barges from St. Louis to render succor. In commemoration of this event, the year 1785 was characterized in ancient chronicles and by the French settlers, as *L'Année des Grandes Eaux*—"The Year of the Great Waters;" and, for more than half a century, until the summer of 1844, its title to that supremacy remained undisputed.

New Orleans, at this early period, was the only mart for St. Louis at which to obtain the luxuries or comforts of life, and, in exchange for the products of the fur trade, to secure the materials and munitions for carrying it on. The only medium through which this commerce could then be transacted—the only mode of navigating the great western waters was the keel-boat and the barge; and one may easily conceive the toil and tediousness, attending a passage of three or four months of a heavily-laden boat against the mighty current of the terrible Mississippi, for twelve hundred miles. But, as if these obstacles and perils were not sufficient, they were greatly increased by attacks of robbers, who stationed themselves at favourable points along the banks where the current was most rapid, or the stream most shallow or most obstructed by snags. One favorite haunt of these maurauders was the Grand Tower, about sixty miles below St. Louis, and another at the mouth of Cottonwood creek; and, among the robbers, the most noted of the leaders were two men named Magilbray and Culburt. In the spring of 1787, it is related that a barge from New Orleans, richly laden, belonging to a merchant of St. Louis, M. Beausoliel, having passed the mouth of the fatal creek in safety impelled by a favorable breeze, two days later was cut off by the robbers, who had gone up by land, and was boarded at an island ever since known as Beausoliel's Island. The prow of the barge was at once directed down stream towards the robbers' haunt; but, before it was reached, the crew, led on by a faithful negro slave belonging to Beausoliel, named Cacasotte, through a well-devised stratagem, had surprised their captors and thrown them into the river. The barge then returned in all haste to New Orleans and reported its adventure. To guard against such dangers in future, the Intendant of the Province, Don Estevan Miro, ordered that all barges destined for the upper country the ensuing spring, should start in company for mutual defence. These barges proved to be ten in number, and the prow of each was mounted with a swivel, and all their crews were amply armed. Approaching the notorious spot, the robbers were perceived beneath the trees on the shore; but they immediately fled, leaving a rich hoard of merchandise, arms, and supplies behind. The robber-band thus broken up never again came together, and the remarkable event of the arrival of ten boats at St. Louis at one time, distinguished the year 1788 as an era in the history of western navigation; and it was ever after called *L'Année des Dix Batteux*—"The year of the Ten Boats."

In the summer of 1792, it is recorded, that the honey-bee, that busy harbinger and constant companion of civilization, made his first appearance on the western shore of the Mississippi. Ten years later, on the 15th of May, 1801, the small-pox first appeared; and so fatal and extensive were its ravages, that another epoch in the chronology of St. Louis became *L'Année de la Picotte*—"The year of the Small-pox."

The commerce of St. Louis, and of the whole Western Valley, was, at this time greatly retarded in its progress, by a controversy between Spain and the United States, with respect to the free navigation of the Mississippi. From the treaty of September 3, 1783, between England, France, Spain, and the United States, for a period of twelve consecutive years almost incessant dissension on this subject prevailed. At length, by the treaty of San Lorenzo, of October 20, 1795, it was stipulated by Spain, that the whole river, from its source to the sea, should be free to the people of the United States, and that the port of New Orleans should for ten years be a place of deposit for their produce and merchandise. But difficulties again arose: "the right of deposit" was repeatedly suspended in course of the ensuing seven or eight years, and the indignation of the Western people was deeply roused. Meantime, Spain had succumbed to the power of Napoleon; and, to efface the ignominy of the Peace of Paris of 1762, by which France had resigned nearly all her vast possessions on the North American continent to England and Spain, it was stipulated, in the third article of the treaty of San Ildefonso, October 1, 1800, that, in consideration of the Kingdom of Tuscany, valued at twenty millions of dollars, Spain should retrocede to France the whole of Louisiana. An army of twenty-five thousand men and a large fleet were at once got ready by the First Consul to secure his new acquisition; but he soon had the sagacity to discover, that this would be impossible; and to prevent that vast territory from falling into the hands of England, his foe, by a treaty of April 30, 1803, he sold it to Mr. Jefferson for fifteen millions of dollars. On Tuesday, the 20th of November, in accordance with the treaty of San Ildefonso, Louisiana was formally delivered by Governor Salcedo and the Marquis of Casa Calvo, in behalf of Spain, to Don Pedro Clement Lausat, commissioner in behalf of France; who, on the morning of Monday, the 20th of December, just one month later, formally delivered the same to W. C. C. Claiborne, Governor of the "Territory of Orleans," and Gen. James Wilkinson, commandant of the troops, in behalf of the United States.

And thus ceased the Spanish rule in Louisiana, after a duration of more than the third of a century. Against this cession, Spain, through her Envoy at Washington, had entered a solemn protest, declaring the act null and void, inasmuch as the cession to France had been made upon express condition that the province should never be alienated. But the remonstrance had been disregarded by Mr. Jefferson; Congress had been convened in extra session; the treaty had been ratified, October 21, 1803; commissioners had been appointed to receive the territory, and strong bodies of Federal troops had been marched to the spot to secure the prize, and to put down all apprehended opposition.

On the evening of Saturday, the 9th day of July, 1803, the first rumor of the retrocession of Louisiana to France reached St. Louis; and the sensation which it caused was vivid and by no means pleasant. The first official intelligence of the double transfer, to which she, in common with all the rest of Louisiana, had been subjected, was not received, however, until some six months later, when it arrived through the medium of a letter from Amos Stoddard, Captain of United States Artillery at Kaskaskia, addressed to Don Carlos Dehault Delassus, Lieut. Governor of Upper Louisiana. It was dated February 18, 1804, and announced the reception by express from New Orleans of various despatches of the previous month, relative to the late retrocession and cession of the province. Such of these despatches as were addressed to the Governor were forwarded to him by Stoddard, who stated that the troops under his command would, in a few days, embark in barges for St. Louis, and himself would precede them by land, in order to make arrangements for their disposition. This letter was replied to very graciously on the 20th by Delassus, in the French language, the Spanish not being intelligible to Stoddard, acknowledging the reception of orders from New Orleans in the despatches forwarded, to deliver the province into the hands of Stoddard, as agent and commissioner on the part of the French Republic; and stating that he had forwarded additional orders by the bearer to the commandants of the minor posts at Ste. Genevieve, Cape Girardeau, New Madrid, and New Bourbon, for their immediate surrender. On Saturday, the 25th, Stoddard reached St. Louis and presented Delassus a formal demand for delivery of the territory with all its posts and dependencies; to which demand the Governor as formally replied, that he was ready to deliver possession "any day and any hour that might be named." On Friday, the 9th of March, therefore, the delivery, by appointment, took place, and a document confirmatory of the fact was signed by Stoddard and Delassus, three copies being in the Spanish language and three in the English. On the following day, the post and province were formally delivered by Amos Stoddard, Agent for the French Republic, to Amos Stoddard, Agent for the United States, who had been appointed civil and military commandant of the district with all the prerogatives and powers of his Spanish predecessor.

On assuming authority, Captain Stoddard issued an address to the inhabitants well calculated to conciliate, assuring them of the interest of the United States in their welfare, and that they might rely on its equity and liberality. At first, however, the change was viewed with regret and greeted with lamentations. To the mild and patriarchal rule of Spain, during more than thirty years, the simple French villagers had become warmly attached; and, though nearly a twelvemonth had elapsed since they had looked forward to a change, they had by no means succeeded in becoming reconciled to the anticipation by the lapse of time.

If we inquire into the general aspect and character of St. Louis on the 9th of March, 1804, when she came under the authority of the United States, we shall find them very different from what they now are, exactly fifty years after that event. Then, along the whole length of the village, extended a bold and beetling cliff, sixty or eighty feet high, overhanging a low flat beach of sand. The Mississippi was little more than half a mile wide; and neither Duncan's Island nor Bloody Island had any existence. The ledge on which the latter lies was covered with water; and a dozen years later a flourishing corn-field, owned by Gen. Rector, occupied the soil where since has flowed the Illinois *shute*. In 1818, the eastern channel began forming, and since that time the landing in front of the town has been projected into the stream several hundred yards. Above the bluff which bordered the river extended two broad banks, steppes, or plateaux, and on the first of these was sparsely sprinkled the town along three parallel streets—*La Rue Principale,* now Main Street—*La Rue de L'Eglise,* where stood the old log church, now Second Street, and *La Rue des Granges,* where stood the barns, now Third Street. Intersecting these streets were others, as high up as Oak Street, where stood the Half-Moon fortification, and as low down as the present Convent Street, or the fort at the bridge, the whole town being circled by a stockade and towers along the brow of the second bank, beyond which on the broad rolling prairie were spread the commons, out-lots and common fields, according to the custom of these old French villages, embracing several thousand acres. These commons and common-fields, it may be observed, were some years since cut up into lots and disposed of on perpetual lease to the highest bidder; and the Carondelet, St. Charles, and other commons have shared a like fate. Above the town were three or four extraordinary groups of ancient mounds, proving that the site of St. Louis, like those of Cincinnati, Chilicothe, Portsmouth, Marietta, Ste. Genevieve, and of other places, was a favorite resort of the early dwellers in this pleasant land. Of all these monuments of the past at St. Louis, however, one only now remains, called by the old French, *La Butte de Terre,* and since known as the Big Mound, because the largest of all; and this it has been recently proposed to the city to purchase, for preservation, and as the site for a contemplated statue of Henry Clay. The number of houses in St. Louis at that time was about one hundred and twenty, many of them being of logs, chinked and plastered, "miserably constructed, comfortless and tasteless," —some of stone being of large size, surrounded with loop-holed walls, like ancient chateaus, and all with the heavy roofs and broad galleries, by which the buildings of these early French and Spanish villages were characterized. The first brick dwelling was erected in 1814. The first street was paved in 1818. It was Market Street, between Front and Main—the limestone rock being planted on edge. *Pain Court,* "Short Bread," or "Short Loaf of Bread," a name suggestive of want, was still a nick-name applied to St. Louis by her neighbors, especially by the villagers of Carondelet, whose residence, in a like spirit of badinage, was called *Vide Poche,* "Empty Pocket," a soubriquet it yet retains. The Government House of the Province stood at the south-east corner of what are now Main and Walnut Streets. The primitive Church, already alluded to, was a structure of some sixty feet by thirty, of hewn logs planted upright, with a steep, heavy projecting roof, surmounted by a belfry, and that by a huge iron cock as a weather-vane, standing on what is now Second Street, between Market and Walnut, and giving, as we have seen, a name to the street. The first plan of *St. Louis des Illinois,* as it was then called, drawn by order of Laclede, in 1764, by Auguste Chouteau, is yet extant, as is, also, another of the place as fortified by Cruzat, in 1780, certified by the same old resident in 1825.

The population of Upper Louisiana at this time, according to a census taken by order of Delassus a few years before, amounted to more than five thousand whites, nearly nine hundred slaves, and about a hundred free blacks. The marriages averaged annually about forty, the deaths about fifty, the births about two hundred. The population of St. Louis was nine hundred and twenty-five, while that of Ste. Genevieve was nine hundred and forty-nine, and that of New Madrid seven hundred and eighty-two. Indeed, Ste. Genevieve, at that time, on account of its superior mineral and agricultural advantages, as well as its livelier business and larger population, presented attractions to the immigrant which the Capital itself could not boast. Many of the villagers were voyageurs, trappers and traders, absent most of the year up the Mississippi and Missouri, and the commerce consisted chiefly of peltry and furs, designed for the markets of Montreal and Quebec, whence they were shipped for Europe. Four years were required for the returns of goods; and yet, though the freight and charges amounted to a hundred per cent., the profits are said to have reached three times as much! The trade of the Missouri river, which was the most valuable, is said to have demanded $60,000 in goods every year, for furs worth more than three times that sum, during each one of the fifteen successive years prior to 1804!

This fur trade commenced at a very early period—long before the founding of St. Louis. As early as 1792, a Scotchman, named Todd, formed a company designed to monopolize the business, and Baptiste Trudeau, the first school-master at St. Louis, was a fur-trader as well as a teacher. The first American who ever traversed the Plains to Santa Fè was James Pursley, a trapper, in 1802; and his three years of adventure among the savages are little less than a romance. At the time of the transfer there were but two American families resident in St. Louis. Groceries were supplied from New Orleans by barges. The trip required from four to six months, and the arrival or departure of a barge was an event. The trip from Louisville to St. Louis, by barge, demanded a month! The small currency was peltry, or "Peltry Bons"—small bills, payable in peltry; and a grasp of the hand sealed a bargain as securely as a bond; while a happier, more hospitable, contented and virtuous community never existed, as all chronicles concur in declaring, than that of St. Louis and the neighboring villages, cut off from all the rest of the world by a thousand miles of land and water.

By act of Congress of the 26th of March, 1804, about three weeks after Stoddard's arrival at St Louis, the "Territory of Orleans" was constituted a District of the United States, under the name of the "District of Louisiana." The Spanish laws were, by the same act, expressly continued in force, until altered or repealed by legislative authority; and this provision, confirmed by acts in 1805 and 1812, remained unaltered until, by the Territorial Legislature of Missouri, in 1816, the Common Law of England was introduced, "to supply deficiencies." By virtue of the same act of Congress of 1804, Gen. Harrison, Governor of Indiana, aided by the judges of that territory, on the 1st of October of that year, commenced a code for the government of the District, and, in the following spring, the first American court west of the Mississippi was held at St. Louis, in the ancient mansion of Auguste Chouteau. In March, 1805, the District of Louisiana was constituted the Territory of Louisiana, and a Supreme Court was created, with Messrs. Lucas, Coburn and Easton as judges; and, in 1812, its name was again changed, and it was called the "Territory of Missouri." In 1805, Gen. James Wilkinson, the Commander-in-chief of the army of the United States, superseded Gen. Harrison as Governor of Upper Louisiana, and commandants were appointed for the posts of St. Louis, St. Charles, Ste. Genevieve and Cape Girardeau, who administered the laws until the organization of courts. In 1806, the Fort of Belle Fontaine, on the south side of the Missouri, near its mouth, was established, but was partially abandoned in 1807, when Gen. Wilkinson and his troops were ordered down the river to arrest the conspiracy of Burr, and wholly so on the 4th of July, 1826, when the garrison first took possession of Jefferson Barracks, a dozen miles below the town.

The first Governor of Missouri Territory was Gen. William Clarke; the first delegate to Congress was Edward Hempstead; and the first Legislature in Missouri sat in a house on Main street, between Walnut and Elm, yet standing, in the winter of 1812–

13; while the first newspaper was the "Missouri Gazette," issued on the 1st day of July, 1808, on a sheet of writing-paper, by Joseph Charless, printer of the laws. In 1809, St. Louis was first incorporated as a town.

Meantime, American immigration from the east had poured steadily in, and, in 1810, the population of St. Louis had increased to fourteen hundred souls, of which number about three hundred were Americans, four hundred slaves and free blacks, and the residue French and Spanish, with a few Indians. Six or seven houses were built that year; rents were high, dwellings were crowded, tenements were almost impossible to obtain; there was a printing office and twelve mercantile stores; the imports of merchandize for the year were estimated at $250,000; the great lead, peltry, and agricultural mart of the country was here, and here were made their respective outfits; while the troops of Belle Fontaine are said to have caused an annual circulation of more than $60,000. Two years later, war with England let loose on the frontier the merciless savage; and St. Charles, and settlements still farther west, severely suffered. But, with the return of peace, the tide of immigration set strongly in from Kentucky and Tennessee; and the French town of St. Louis, with its long, narrow streets, parallel to the river, its French cottages and Spanish towers, began to feel the effects of the language, laws, usages, manners, and customs, and the enterprising spirit of the Anglo-Saxon race; while the gradual extinction of Indian title to the western lands by five distinct treaties, between the years 1808 and 1818, encouraged the immigrant still more. The census of 1815, therefore, gave the population at two thousand, and that of 1820, at nearly five, while improvement and commerce had proportionally augmented. In 1818, for example, a hundred houses were erected, and the amount raised by taxes was nearly $3,000. The paying of taxes, however, proved hardly more agreeable to the French villager than the voting for rulers; while the American laws and courts, and the customs generally, were far from agreeable.

It was on the 2d day of August, 1817, that the first steamboat reached St. Louis. The boat was built at Louisville, was propelled by a low-pressure engine, had but one chimney, was commanded by Capt. Jacob Reed, and was called the "General Piké," a name ever since so popular for steamboats on the Ohio. It was about the hour of noon when the long-looked-for *Bateau au fer* approached the town; and as she landed at the lower end of the place, at the foot of the present Myrtle Street, the simple French villagers were hardly less amazed at the strange monster, than were a band of Indians who were on a visit to St. Louis, whom no persuasion could induce to approach nearer to it than the brow of the hill where the Court House now stands. The second boat which arrived was the "Constitution," Capt. R. P. Gayard, October 2d of the same year. Two years later, the "Independence," Capt. Nelson, was the first steamboat to ascend the Missouri river, which had, originally, been supposed navigable only by pirogues. On the 19th of May, 1819, the "Independence" reached the town of Old Franklin, a distance of two hundred miles, in seven "sailing days," and was saluted by cannon by the inhabitants. On the 5th of June she was again at St. Louis and took in freight for Louisville. Twelve years later, in 1829, the "Yellow-Stone" ascended the Missouri to the Falls, followed by the "Assinaboine," and the "occupation" of the keel, and the barge, and the Mackinaw batteau was forever "gone."

The steamboat "Harriet," Capt. Armitage, reached St. Louis from New Orleans on the 2d of June of the same year, after a trip of twenty-seven days—now accomplished in four. The Steam-King had now made that advent in the Western Valley which was destined to revolutionize its whole history; and the barge, and the boatman, disappeared never to return.

The Fur Trade, as a depot for which the site of St. Louis had been originally selected by Laclede, continued for many years the chief interest and occupation of her commerce. As early as 1804, when Lewis and Clarke were sent by the United States Government on their celebrated expedition to the head waters of the great Western Rivers, the trapper and the hunter had preceded them. In 1808, the Missouri Fur Company was formed by Pierre Chouteau and others, with a capital of $40,000, and was finally dissolved in 1812. Other companies succeeded, and the names of John Jacob Astor and William H. Ashley are conspicuous in the annals of that lucrative and enterprising trade from 1819 to 1823, even as those of Chouteau, Campbell, Cabanne, Sublette, Pratte, Bent and St. Vrain have been since. The value of the trade during the forty years last past, is estimated to have averaged not less than $250,000 a year. In 1820, the peltries of the American Fur Company are said to have amounted to a million of dollars annually. This Company was incorporated in New York, in 1808, for a term of forty years, with a capital of two millions, and remained under Astor's management until 1834, when he sold out. It was for the accommodation of this extensive and lucrative trade, that some of the massive warehouses of stone, which now ornament the Landing of St. Louis and make its river approach so imposing, were constructed, the cellars supplying the material for the superstructures, some of them becoming thus as many stories deep under ground as they were stories high above.

In 1817, the Missouri Territory having sixty thousand inhabitants, demanded admission into the Union. A strong resistance, on account of her slavery, at once arose. In 1819, Congress cut off the Southern section of the Territory, and organized it as the "Arkansas Territory," containing then, some fourteen thousand inhabitants; but, in 1820, the Territory of Missouri was authorized to form a constitution, preliminary to admission into the Union, and a Convention of forty delegates from fifteen counties, met at St. Louis on the 12th of June, and, after a session of five weeks, on the 19th of July, completed its labors. A General Assembly was then chosen, and Alexander McNair was elected first Governor. The population was then upwards of sixty-six thousand, of which number, more than ten thousand were slaves, and less than five thousand were citizens of St. Louis. The famous "Missouri Question"—the question whether Missouri, with her slaves, should be admitted into the confederacy—for two years convulsed the Union from one end to the other, and, at one time, was even thought to threaten its dismemberment: but the fiery ordeal was at length passed; a spirit of compromise and concession triumphed; on the 2d of March, 1821, Missouri was admitted; and, on the 19th of August, of the same year, on compliance with the terms, she became by the President's proclamation, the twenty-first of the United States.

The current of immigration to Missouri now flowed in from the Northern and Western States, and commenced, also, from Europe. Commerce, agriculture, trade, received new life, and, in 1830, the State had a population of more than a hundred and forty thousand souls, and St. Louis of nearly six thousand. The town of St. Charles was the temporary capital of the State for several years and until 1826, when Jefferson City was made the permanent seat of Government. But, although the rising emporium of the West had now a population six times as large as when she became a portion of the Republic, a quarter of a century before, and, although, some years previous, in 1822, she had been advanced to the dignity of a city, she was still only "a little French City," and so continued for some years to come. Indeed, as late as the summer of 1836, when the writer of this hasty sketch first repaired to St. Louis, he recorded the fact, that, despite all the improvements of the last few years, she yet remained emphatically only a little *French* City. "There is about the place," continues this record of seventeen years since, "a cheerful village air, a certain *rus in urbe*, to which the grenadier preciseness of most of our cities is the antipodes. There yet remains in St. Louis much to remind one of its early days. Until within a few years there was no such thing as a row of houses; all were disjoined and at a considerable distance from each other; and every edifice, however central, could boast its humble *stoop*, its front-door plat, bedecked with shrubbery and flowers, and protected from the inroads of intruding man or beast by its own tall stockade. All this is now confined to the Southern, or French section of the city—a right Rip Van Winkle-looking region, where each little steep-roofed cottage yet presents its broad piazza, and the cosey settee before the door, beneath the tree shade, with the fleshy old burghers soberly luxuriating on an evening pipe, their dark-eyed, brunette daughters at their side. There is a delightful air of old-fashioned comfortableness in all this, that reminds us of nothing we have seen in our own country, but of much of the antiquated villages, of which we have been told, in the land beyond the waters. There is, indeed, a venerable air about its narrow streets and the ungainly edifices of one portion of St. Louis—the steep-roofed stone cottage of the Frenchman, and the tall stuccoed dwelling of the Don, not often beheld. The modern section of the city, with its regular streets and lofty edifices, which, within the past fifteen years has risen under the active hand of the northern immigrant, presents a striking contrast to the old." The castellated mansions of the brothers

Chouteau, with their enclosures of heavy masonry, with loop-holes and watch-towers for defence, though somewhat encroached on by the march of improvement, were yet to be seen, monuments of an earlier era, still inhabited by the posterity of their builders. Of the old Spanish towers of Cruzat, which, in 1780, encircled the village, however, not a vestige remained, the great earthquakes of 1811, by which the whole Western Valley, and especially New Madrid, had been powerfully shaken, having aided in toppling the old ruins to the ground. Roy's Tower, however, on the river-bank, at the upper extremity of the city, still remained, as well as most of those remarkable Mounds of the ancient tomb-builders, in the northern suburbs, for which St. Louis was long so celebrated, and to which she owes her appropriate appellation of the "Mound City." They were numerous, and their site was, as is usual, a commanding one, on the second bank, plateau, or steppe, looking proudly down on the Mississippi, parallel to which they lay.

But all now is changed, and has been so this ten years. The Chouteau mansions are both gone, and their sites are occupied by lofty blocks of stores. Gone too is Roy's Tower, and gone are all the mounds save one; and that—the proudest of them all, the ravages of men and the elements are rapidly wasting away. It may be remarked that there were hundreds of these mounds, large and small, in St. Louis county when first settled; and, within five miles of the city, on the American bottom opposite, in Illinois, were hundreds more, all of them, so far as examined, containing human remains, and vestiges of coal, pottery and fire. Within the present century an Osage chieftain dying on a visit to St. Louis was interred by his followers on the summit of the "Big Mound." Very different was the view from this ancient watch-tower—this Indian vidette, then from what it is now. Then, the eye swept over a boundless expanse of tree-tops, even to the horizon on the north and west, while, on the south, over a green grove and groups of lesser mounds, rose the only spire which the town could boast, with its gilded ball and cross. Chouteau's Pond, with its massive and moss-grown Mill shaded by venerable sycamores, was then a romantic water-sheet. But the water became impure and unhealthy because of manufactories on the banks, and, by city authority, it was recently drained, and will soon, doubtless, be filled up, divided by streets and covered with buildings. The old Mill with its aged sycamores may yet remain; but the doom of both is sealed. The "Prairie House" and the "U. S. Arsenal" were then a pleasant evening's drive from the city; now, they are almost within the city limits. Carondelet was then a wretched Creole "Empty Pocket" hamlet, approached by an execrable road winding over hills and among sink-holes; now, the road is a turnpike, and will soon be a railroad, and the French Vide Poche is a promising town. The extensive sand-bar, which subsequently increased so alarmingly along the southern front of the landing, had then, for some years, been accumulating, threatening utter ruin to the harbor, and to render St. Louis "an inland town." To obviate a fate so disastrous, petition after petition was sent to Washington, and appropriation after appropriation was voted by Congress. And survey after survey was made, and plan after plan was devised by engineers; and the shores of Illinois and Bloody Island bristled with revetments, and wing-dams and stoccades; and thousands on thousands of dollars were sunk in the river; and all in vain—all the works, year after year, being swept off by the annual floods—the obstructions becoming constantly more alarming, until, at length, the city authorities themselves energetically seized the old Father of Waters by the mane, and bridled him by means of massive dykes and dams from the foot of the Island to the Illinois shore. These dykes and improvements are now above high-water mark, and are deemed quite secure; the intervening space is rapidly filling up, and, in a few years, "Gen. Rector's corn-field" of 1816 may be completely restored where so long has flowed the main channel of the largest river in the world. The change of current from the Missouri to the Illinois shore was attributed, and perhaps justly, to the protrusion of the landing of St. Louis into the stream, and the long line of steamboats and floating docks constantly there. A few years ago, also, the Missouri threatened to cut through the soft alluvion of the American bottom opposite its mouth, and to seek its ancient channel five miles distant, along the Illinois Bluffs: but, last spring, the capricious flood opened for itself a new outlet across the Mamelle Prairie, higher up and nearer to Alton, and the peril seems suspended for a time if not entirely obviated forever.

The idea of bridgeing the Mississippi, has been more than once suggested; and, in 1839, in compliance with a request of the City Council, the celebrated Charles Ellet of Philadelphia, since architect of the wire Suspension bridge at Niagara Falls, reported plans and estimates for a similar structure over the Father of Waters. By one of his three propositions, the bridge was to cross the river from the foot of Market Street by three arches. Its length was to be three thousand feet; its height above low water, seventy; its two towers two hundred feet high; its capacity to sustain about seven thousand tons, and its cost about $700,000. The Wheeling bridge, since erected, is only about a thousand feet long, a hundred feet high, and its cost was about $200,000; yet this is the most remarkable bridge of the kind in the world, that at Fribourg, in Switzerland, not excepted. In the winter of 1849, the Legislature of Illinois chartered a company to bridge the Mississippi at St. Louis, and also at the Grand Tower, sixty miles below; but nothing further was done. The task would be now comparatively easy at St. Louis, since Bloody Island has been connected with Illinois by means of a road over the dyke. A bridge for the Rock Island Railroad over the Mississippi at Fort Armstrong, fifteen hundred feet long, with a draw for boats, is to be completed at the close of 1854, for $175,000.

But, marked as were the improvements of St. Louis in the lapse of the thirty years which intervened between 1804 and 1834, it has been, nevertheless, within the lapse of the twenty years which have since ensued, that her vast resources have been chiefly developed; and the summer of 1836 may be named as the period from which her unparalleled advancement may be dated, more justly perhaps, than from any other. Her population, which in 1810 was less than two thousand, and in 1820 less than five thousand, and in 1830 less than seven thousand, was in 1850, nearly eighty-three thousand, and in 1853, about one hundred thousand, showing the unparalleled average increase of at least five thousand souls each year, during each of the last twenty consecutive years!

From 1833 to 1837, the population of six thousand doubled, and from 1837 to 1841, it more than doubled again, reaching thirty thousand souls! In 1835, the population was eight thousand, and in 1845, it was thirty-six thousand! Well has it been said, therefore, that "the increase of population in St. Louis, is unparalleled in any city in the Union, or in the world."

Much of this increase is, it is true, to be attributed to immigration from Europe, and especially from Germany; yet a very fair proportion is of native born Americans from the older states of the confederation.

With the events most prominent in the history of St. Louis during the eighteen or twenty years last past, nearly every one is so familiar, that they need but be recalled by recapitulation. The burning of a negro, whose hands were crimson with the blood of two atrocious murders, in 1836, and the hanging of four negroes guilty of murder and arson, in 1841; the unparalleled flood of 1844, which submerged the whole landing of St. Louis and the whole American Bottom; the terrific conflagration of 1849, which destroyed millions of property, and the yet more terrific pestilence which ensued the same year, destroying thousands of lives—these are events associated with the name of St. Louis in the minds of all who have read the newspapers of the day.

In 1847, on the 15th day of February, the eighty-third anniversary of the landing of Laclede and the founding of the city, was celebrated in most imposing style, with salvoes of artillery, with a civic and military procession, with an address to an immense concourse in front of the Court House, and with a grand public dinner, the day being concluded with a public ball,—in all which festivities the aged Pierre Chouteau—the only man then surviving who had witnessed the scenes commemorated, but now no more, together with several early settlers, also since deceased—participated.

In 1848, the Railroad enterprise, now a feature of the place, took its rise. On the 4th of July, 1851, ground was broken with imposing ceremonies at the eastern terminus, at St. Louis, of a road designed to extend to Kansas, the State line, a distance of three hundred miles, and peradventure, to the shores of the Pacific; and, on the 19th of July, 1853, with ceremonies equally imposing, the first division of forty miles was opened, and hundreds of citizens were transported in cars of St. Louis manufacture, and by means of a locomotive of St. Louis construction; while at the close of 1854, the cars will doubtless run to Jefferson City, the State-capital, a distance of nearly ninety miles further. Meantime, while extending one iron arm towards the Pacific, St. Louis has been extending the other towards the Atlantic. In December, 1851, a contract was closed between the Ohio and Mississippi Railroad Company and the celebrated Seymour, to construct a road from St. Louis to Cincinnatti, a distance of some three hundred and thirty miles, for some nine millions of dollars; and on the 7th of February, 1852, ground was broken at Illinoistown, opposite the city, with appropriate pomp. By New Year's day, 1854, cars will be rolling over a portion of this road, and by the 1st day of July, they will have reached Vincennes; and, when wholly completed, the road will constitute "a link in a line, the extent of which neither has been, nor can be, equalled on the earth,"—a line two thousand miles long on the east to Halifax, and more than two thousand miles long on the west to San Francisco, with branches numberless, to every city north and south, extending thousands of miles more!

The advantage to St. Louis of the Railroad Enterprise has already been great; but it is destined to become incalculably greater, when, not only the Atlantic and the Pacific roads, but the Iron Mountain, the Southwestern, the North Missouri, the Hannibal and St. Joseph, as well as the Chicago and Mississippi, and the Illinois Central roads, and numerous others now contemplated, shall have directly or indirectly contributed to render St. Louis second to no city on the Western Continent. Indeed, it has been estimated that when all the routes now contemplated around St. Louis shall have been completed, she will be the nucleus of more railroads than even Boston at present is; while, within ten years, they will have increased her population to half a million, and have made her the mart for eight times as many more! That this is to be the destiny of this remarkable city seems fixed even by nature herself. Geographically the centre of the Continent and of the great Western Valley, with its fifty thousand miles of boatable water and its hundreds of millions of acres of arable land—situated near the confluence of three of the finest rivers in the world—with a back-country boundless in extent and matchless in fertility—with a climate unsurpassed in mildness and salubrity most of the year—surrounded by fields of coal and iron ample in quantity to supply a world, and by deposits of nearly every species of earth and mineral of which science has taken cognizance—with important government depots and establishments within a dozen miles—with an enterpising, industrious and thrifty population which doubles itself every five years—where is the city which has the promise of St. Louis? If her past affords any criterion on which to base prediction for her future, what may she not thirty years hence have become?

Thirty years ago her population was little less than five thousand, now it is little less than a hundred thousand: then, her revenue from all sources was less than five thousand dollars, now, it amounts to more than half a million, assessed on property valued at a hundred times that amount—though not one of the millionaires now was a millionaire then, and but few tax-payers then are tax-payers now. Then her ancient

"Commons" were probably worth but a few dollars the acre; now, a remnant only, consisting of some twelve hundred acres, is worth a million of dollars, the title to one-half of the same being clear and undoubted. Then, the arrival of boats and barges at her landing, was less than four hundred in a year—now, it is nearer four thousand, while the wharfage fees, from less than two hundred dollars, have become more than fifty thousand dollars. Then, her system of water-works scarcely had existence—now, water forced up by engines a distance of two miles from the river, is distributed by a reservoir containing five millions of gallons, through pipes more than thirty miles in extent, while yet other works are spoken of which shall supply a population of half a million with ten gallons each person, each day. Gas-works were then unknown—but, within the last six years, they have been commenced, and now extend their pipes more than thirty miles.

Real estate, then, on the principal streets was, probably, worth as many dollars per foot as it is now worth hundreds of dollars; for, where it will now bring $500, five years ago it brought only $100; and where it now brings $800, ten years ago it brought only $500. Then, there were but four churches, now there are forty and four; seating nearly forty thousand persons, and worth more than a million of dollars. In 1804, it may be remarked, no religion was tolerated by Spain but the Catholic, which had been the religion of St. Louis since its foundation: and itinerant Methodists and Baptists, who crossed the river from Illinois to preach in private houses, did it at their peril. In 1817, a Presbyterian church of ten members was organized by missionaries, and, in 1828, its church, at the corner of St. Charles and Fourth streets, was dedicated. The edifice was then "in the country,"—its site is now occupied by stores. For many years this was the only Protestant church in St. Louis. Not until 1830, indeed, did any faith but the Catholic prevail. Now, there are a dozen Catholic churches and three times as many Protestant churches, instead of one of each sect. Then, there was a City Hall, worth $20,000, now its site is occupied by structures, rented, perchance, for twice that amount, and worth, perchance, that amount twenty times told. Then, there was neither medical school nor theatre—a temple of science or a temple of art; now, there are three temples of each. The "Republican" newspaper, which now issues an aggregate of reading matter equivalent to more than five hundred pages each week, then, as for years before it had been, was almost the only representative of the press in St. Louis, and issued a semi-weekly sheet of only a few thousand ems. Then there was a Court House worth $14,000, soon there will be one worth half a million. Then, public schools scarcely had existence; now they have a fund of a million and a half—an annual income of more than $40,000, and instruct more than four thousand pupils. Then the value of imports was but a few thousand dollars per annum and the amount of duties but a few hundred; now the foreign value of the former is more than a million of dollars each year, and the aggregate amount of the latter collected thereon is more than $300,000 !

But this wonderful contrast, which might be prolonged to an almost indefinite extent, embracing every branch of business, and every interest of social or civilized life, and which is based on official statistics of undoubted authenticity, has been carried far enough to render this comparative view of the past with the present a reliable prophecy for the future. And, with this prophecy, which demands no sooth-sayer to declare, may this hasty and meagre, yet prolonged tribute to St. Louis, from the pen of one who for many years was one of her citizens, be fittingly brought to a close.

Drawn after Nature

For the Proprietor: Hermann J. Meyer

THE COURT-HOUSE IN St. LOUIS

Published for HERMANN J. MEYER 164 William-Str. NEWYORK.

ST. LOUIS COURT HOUSE.

The first Court House in St. Louis was also the first prison, and both were embraced in one of the earliest fortifications. The edifice was of stone, about forty feet in diameter and twenty in height, circular in shape, and situated on the street now known as Walnut street. It was the largest of the half dozen forts, square or circular, constructed for the defence of the place, under the administration of the Spanish Governor, Don Francisco Cruzat, immediately after the attack of the British and savages in 1780; extending in a semicircle, from Roy's Round Tower, above the town, to the bridge below on Second street, where now stand the Gas Works. A similar structure, which stood at the corner of Main and Oak streets, and was subsequently incorporated into the Missouri Hotel after having been used as a magazine, subserved, for some time, the same purpose. But tribunals and prisons, in the old patriarchal era of St. Louis, were, probably, far less in request than they have since been; and it is perhaps, true, as has been asserted, that, during upwards of thirty years from its first settlement, there was not a single instance of flagrant crime. But, with the increase of population, after the transfer of Louisiana to the United States in 1804, increased civil delinquency, and the means for administering its penalties.

The first general court in and for the district of Louisiana, was opened on Tuesday, the 6th day of May, 1805. Some months prior to this, on the 1st of October, 1804, a law had been made establishing the office of Sheriff, and it was the first of the code of laws enacted for the district under authority of Congress, by General Harrison, Governor of the Territory of Indiana, and Messrs. Davis, Griffin and Vanderburgh, the judges. At the hour of eleven, therefore, on the morning of the 6th of May, the two latter of the judges named, attended by the Sheriff and his deputy, by the little bar of lawyers and a body of citizens, repaired from the tavern to the stone mansion of Col.

Chouteau, to open the first American court west of the Mississippi. This Chouteau Mansion was erected as early as 1764, under the superintendence of Auguste Chouteau, who, a youth, had accompanied Laclede, the founder of the town, from New Orleans. Its site was on Main street, opposite the old Market, where Laclede first landed, and looking down on the river. If we except the earliest log cabins of the primitive settlers, the Chouteau mansion was the first edifice erected in St. Louis. Originally a depot for the Louisiana Fur Company of Pierre Laclede, Maxan & Company, it was but a single story in height; but subsequently, by the decease of Laclede, falling into the possession of Col. Chouteau, it was greatly enlarged and improved. Cellars were excavated by the labors of Indian squaws,—broad galleries on two sides were constructed of plank hewed out of oaken timber; the walnut flooring, which remained sound more than a century, was brought from Fort Chartres when that fortress was evacuated;—the walls and pillars were of massive masonry, plastered with mortar; the entire square was surrounded with strong walls, with loop-holes for defence; the roof was broad and heavy, with dormer windows, and a large iron weathercock on each gable; and the structure itself was nearly a hundred feet long, by some sixty wide, with a portico looking out on a fine garden in the rear. Here lived Auguste Chouteau, from the erection of the edifice in 1764, until his own death, in 1839, a period of sixty years; and here the old mansion itself continued tos tand, a monument of the past, for a year later, until swept away in 1840 by the advancing wave of business and population. A mansion in most respects similar to that of Auguste Chouteau, belonging to his younger brother, Pierre, who died more recently, stood at the upper extremity of Main street; and in one or the other of these long-since-demolished mansions was held the first American court.

A grand jury, consisting of twenty citizens, was impanneled, and was charged at some length, by Judge Vanderburgh, and during their session of three days, from Tuesday until Friday, found three indictments for murder, and presented two Justices of the Peace for irregularity. Of those charged with murder, two, named Hunter and Davis, for killing Clark, were, on trial, acquitted, and one named Dennis, for killing his father-in-law, was convicted of manslaughter,—during a session of fifteen days.

It was about this time that the Sioux brought in an Indian, charged with killing two Canadians. Another Indian, who had long been confined in the fort, was shot while attempting to escape; but, some time afterwards, his body was found some six miles from town, and after the arrival of a pardon from President Madison. As late as 1811, the courts were held in the barracks of the old fort, on the brow of the hill, in one of the towers of which was the prison; and here was confined, and here tried and acquitted, an Indian of the Mascotin tribe, for slaying a Kickapoo woman who had been his wife, and who had deserted him, and whom he subsequently chanced to meet in the streets of St. Louis, and, in his fury, instantly stabbed to the heart.

In 1826 was commenced the construction of a Court House, on the site of the present edifice. It was a neat structure of brick, located in the centre of one of the most central and elevated squares of the city, and contained a large court room above, and one below: also, two smaller apartments on each floor, over each other, appropriated, those above, to jury rooms, and those below to the Sheriff and Probate offices. The building was approached from Fourth street by a broad flight of stone steps, and was entered by an imposing arched entrance; it was also surmounted by a cupola commanding an extensive view. Its cost was fourteen thousand dollars.

The magnificent structure which is now in course of completion was commenced some ten or twelve years ago, and is destined to be one of the most imposing edifices of the kind in the United States. Its cost, when it is finished, will not have been less than half a million of dollars. Its general order is Doric; its material is pressed brick, faced with a species of blue stone dressed, and its site is the centre of the old Court House square. The whole area which pertains to it is, or is to be, enclosed by iron palisades. The space occupied by the plan of the building itself, embraces some fifteen thousand square feet; and the dimensions of the main structure are about one hundred and fifty by seventy feet. The form of the building is a Greek cross, presenting a colonade front, when completed, to each cardinal point of the compass, each front being exactly like the others. The form of the cross is created by a projection of the northern and southern fronts of the edifice, about thirty feet from the main body, while the porticoes of these fronts project about a dozen feet farther. The eastern and western porticoes have the same projection, and extend across the entire width of what may be called the nave; and each portico is approached by massive flights of steps. The basement of the building contains some ten or twelve fire-proof offices, roofed by groined arches, composed of stone and brick, which support the floor of the main building. There are, also, several cisterns in the basement, supplied with water by the city water-works, and communicating with the city sewers. The principal floor is divided into two spacious court rooms, one of which has, for some years, been completed, and occupied by the Circuit Court; and to each belongs a clerk's office, entirely fire-proof. There are also two other rooms, one to be appropriated to the Probate Court and the other to the Law Library. On this floor, likewise, is the Rotunda, occupying the centre of the edifice, at the intersection of the nave and transept of the cross. It is sixty feet in diameter, and, rising above the roof, is surmounted by a heavy dome, at an altitude of about a hundred and thirty feet from the ground. It has three galleries, the first ascended by a spiral staircase of oak and iron, and supported by massive columns of stone, and the two others mounted by side-stairs, and sustained by cast iron columns. This noble Rotunda will accommodate about four thousand persons, and has been for years the scene of most of the mass meetings of St. Louis. The second floor of the edifice is to contain two fine court rooms, one of which has been completed, and in use by the Court of Common Pleas for several years; and to each of these belongs a fire-proof office for the clerk, designed to stand directly over the two fire-proof clerk's offices on the first floor, rendering the north transept of the building which they are to occupy, completely fire-proof from basement to roof—from "turret to foundation-stone." The residue of the space on this floor is to be occupied by jury rooms, while in the trigliph story above, lighted by circular windows, are to be eight other apartments for the same purpose.

The view unfolded to the eye from the dome of the St. Louis Court House has no equal in the valley of the Mississippi. Before you roll the turbid floods of the Father of Waters, as they come sweeping on from the north and go winding away on their far pilgrimage to the sunnier climes of the Mexican sea. Beyond the stream is spread the vast plain of the American Bottom, with flashing lagunes, and smiling farms, and ancient mounds, and island-groves, the whole bounded by the blue line of the distant bluffs; while along the middle of the river stretch the ill-omened sands of the Island of Blood, with their revetements and embankments; and yet more near, the eye is arrested by the city Landing, fringed with its dark forest of steamboat flues. On the north and west extends an undulating plain, sprinkled with farms and country-seats as far as the eye can reach, even until arrested in its sweep by the forests that look away to the setting sun and down on the rolling Missouri, and by the hills and dales of Bellefontaine, the City of the Dead. Southwardly, in dim distance, we view the white cliffs which bound the mighty river; and amidst the dense boughs of heavy forests, catch glimpses of old French hamlets, or of the bright folds of the stripes and stars which float over Jefferson Barracks, or the nearer Arsenal. And there we behold many a stately structure on its bold bluff, overlooking the gliding waters; while away on our right sparkles the surface of the lake; and the shriek of the iron horse tells us that he has already taken up his far journey for the Pacific. And when the eye shall have gazed until it dims with weariness on all this magnificent and boundless landscape—this varied scene of hill and dale, of forest and field, of villa, and cottage, and meadow,—of mound, hamlet, river and lake, it falls upon the babel below, on the roofs which shelter a hundred thousand souls; the broad streets, the bustling marts, the splendid mansions, the stately temples, the smoking manufactories; and it seems but a tale that is told, that the man has but just died who beheld on the site of all this opulence, and power, and population, only a wild and howling waste!

DRAWN AFTER NATURE

For the Proprietor: HERRMANN J. MEYER.

KANSAS

Published for HERRMANN J. MEYER. 164. William-Str. NEWYORK.

KANSAS.

This place is situated on the right bank of the Missouri river, about one mile below the Kansas* river, the mouth of which forms the boundary line between the State of Missouri and the Indian Territory. A small stream, called Turkey creek, which rises a few miles distant, near the Kansas, winds around the point of the bluff seen in the foreground, and enters the Missouri at the upper end of the town site. The land above, at the mouth of the Kansas, is low alluvion, and overflowed in high-water.

The bluff seen in the rear of the large buildings, is an elevation of about one hundred feet, leaving a spacious landing, with a rocky base, a wide street, and room for blocks of store-houses and other buildings. Towards the lower end of the town site, is a wide plain, from which a ravine furnishes a pathway to the back country, with a convenient grade to the top of the bluff, where a beautiful plateau extends to some distance.

The ox-team and large wagon seen approaching the ferry, gives indication of one of the advantages of this town. It is one of the principal points on the Missouri for the outfit of the caravans of traders and emigrants, on their journey over the plains and mountains, to the far-west. Here many thousands congregate in the spring season, to make preparations for their long line of march towards California, Salt Lake, New Mexico and Oregon. Artisans supply them with wagons and gearing, stores furnish groceries and provisions, and farmers throughout the western part of Missouri are here with mules, horses, oxen and cows, for their teams. Here too, are found "black legs," and other sharpers, with spotted bits of pasteboard, and other contrivances to filch the money and outfit from the wild and thoughtless. This, and several other towns along the turbid Missouri, and on the confines of the Indian country, are places of business and bustle, frolicking and trading, during the spring season.

* The sound of this word by the Indian tribe, that gives the name, is *Kauzau*, and the Indians, by abbreviation, re called *Kaws*.

Six miles in the rear, and directly on the boundary of the Indian country, is the pleasant village of Westport, containing about 700 inhabitants. In the vicinity and some distance within the territory is the region of fresh forage on the prairie for the teams and other animals of the migrating parties. Here may be seen in the season of spring, for several weeks in succession, caravans *en bivouac*, while providing their outfit, or waiting for their friends behind. The early "movers" are here by the first of April, and continue to arrive in steamboats, or in wagons overland, until some time in May. The time of starting depends on the season. They must wait until food for their teams has grown on the plains, in the interior of Nebraska. And then, as a matter of mutual convenience, small companies, as they get ready, start in advance of others. While one party are seen striking their tents and entering on the broad beaten path of an almost endless length, another party arrive—pitch their tents, "hobble" out their teams, light up their camp-fires, and make their first essay in nomadic life.

The sketch of Kansas in the engraving was taken about three years since, since which the town has been much enlarged, and the population increasd to more than 2000. In the immediate vicinity, the surface of the country is undulating, the soil rich, and where not already cultivated, it is covered with heavy forest timber, consisting of walnut, hickory, oaks of various species, linden, hackberry, sugar maple, and other kinds. This belt of timber is from three to six miles wide, and borders on the vast prairies which extend to the western mountains.

DRAWN AFTER NATURE

For the Proprietor: HERRMANN J. MEYER.

ROCK ISLAND CITY

(ILLINOIS)

Published for HERRMANN J. MEYER. 164 William-Str. NEW YORK.

ROCK ISLAND CITY.

Rock Island City is the capital of Rock Island County, in the State of Illinois. It is situated on the west bank of the Mississippi river, at the foot of Rock Island, about one hundred miles south of Galena, and three hundred and twenty-five miles above St. Louis. The city-plat is extended over the gently undulating bottom lands, at the junction of the Rock and Mississippi rivers, covering an area of the most liberal dimensions. In 1836 it contained a few scattered habitations only, and was called Stephenson; and the same year, the old Sac and Fox village-plat, two miles distant, upon Rock river, was surveyed into lots, and named Rock Island City. The pecuniary disasters of that period, and other causes, prevented the contemplated transformation of the ancient Indian capital into a civilized town; and soon after, Stephenson assumed the name first given to the spot whereon Black Hawk was born, and which, for a century, had been the metropolis of his progenitors.

Twenty-five years ago, this locality, and the region round about, were in the possession and occupation of the Indians—the nearest eastern frontier settlements in Illinois had not then approached within sixty miles. It was in this favorite locality of the Sacs and Foxes, and upon which the God of nature had impressed the broad seal of his approbation, that these Native Americans built their capital city, which was the cherished abode of Black Hawk, Keokuk and their fathers, for an hundred years. Here, upon a lovely elevation overlooking the confluence of the Rock and Mississippi rivers, was their ancient cemetery—here their corn-fields, pleasant hunting-grounds, and clear, swift-running waters, abounding in delicious fish—and here, upon the beautiful Rock Island, was the dwelling place of their Great and Good Spirit.

To obtain prematurely the possession of this desirable locality, and expel the Indians therefrom, the United States violated the spirit, if not the letter, of a solemn treaty;

and to retain their cherished city and their rightful privileges of hunting and fishing, Black Hawk and his 500 warriors, bravely encountered an army of 3500 American troops, which resulted in the slaughter of some four or five hundred Indian men, women, and children, about two hundred Americans, and an expenditure of nearly two millions of dollars.

Rock Island City is now a considerable town, rapidly increasing in population and business importance, and destined to become one of the largest cities on the Mississippi river. It has its steamboats, flouring-mills, manufactories, machine-shops, and railroad depots; it is here that the iron rails, extending west from the Atlantic coast, first reached the Father of Rivers, and it is here that the Great River is being spanned by a magnificent Railroad bridge, having arches 250 feet in length, with Rock Island for its central pier. The city and its surroundings are eminently attractive, and few localities are associated with historical and traditional incidents as interesting and enduring.

DRAWN AFTER NATURE

For the Proprietor: HERRMANN J. MEYER.

JEFFERSON CITY

(MISSOURI - RIVER)

Published for HERRMANN J. MEYER. 164. William-Street. NEWYORK.

JEFFERSON CITY.

The capital of the State of Missouri, like the capital of ancient Rome, may be said to be founded on seven hills. It is situated in Cole county, on the south bank of the Missouri, nine miles above the mouth of the Osage, one hundred and thirty-four miles west of St. Louis, and nearly a thousand miles west of Washington city. The spot, embracing about twenty-five hundred acres of land, was granted by Congress as a seat of government for the State; and, on the first day of October, 1826, it was removed hither from its temporary site at St. Charles. Its only claim to be a capital is its central situation; and the sale of its lots has aided in the construction of its public buildings. Its location is elevated, made up of hills and dales, and abounding in conspicuous sites for individual mansions. A few houses are sprinkled along the river bank, but most of the buildings stand on the main street of the town, upon the bluffs. The population is about three thousand. The public buildings are the State Penitentiary, an extensive establishment, which is leased to the highest bidder; the Governor's house, a neat mansion of brick, looking down on the river, and a State Capitol of stone. This imposing edifice was commenced many years since; and, although vast sums have been expended towards its completion, it is still far from being complete. The ground-floor is occupied by the Public Offices, while the floor above is appropriated to the House of Representatives on the north side of the rotunda, and the Senate Chamber on the south. There are, also, several smaller apartments, for the clerks, and a room somewhat larger, in the rear, containing the library. In this chamber for several years, was deposited a full-length portrait of Senator Benton, though it is now, probably, suspended in the Hall of the House. Here also, we believe, are deposited the archives of the Historical Society of Missouri, established some six or eight years ago.

The view from the bluffs on which the Capitol stands, and especially from the dome of the Capitol itself, is extensive and imposing. Away from the west comes sweeping on the turbid Missouri, and is beheld, gliding along the base of the cliff, mile after mile, as it rolls impetuously onward to join its rival, the Mississippi. The river-reach commanded from this point, both above and below, is one of the grandest and most extensive in the West; and boats are seen from the windows of the Capitol approaching the city, breasting the mighty current or hurried along by its force, long before they reach the landing. On the south and east extends the city sprinkled about on its numberless hills; and among the tasteful mansions that of the Governor is most conspicuous. On the west, the eye roams over a broken and undulating landscape of hill and forest, diversified by an occasional farm-house, enlivened by orchards and cultivated fields. On the opposite shore, across the stream, is spread out an extensive bottom, with an occasional dwelling and patches of timber for several miles, bounded by the line of bluffs beyond. Here lies the great county of Callaway, one of the richest, largest, and most fertile in the State,—well-timbered, well-watered and undulating, with its bountiful products of corn, tobacco, and wheat, its thousand farms, its six hundred square miles of territory, its fourteen thousand inhabitants, and its seat of justice, the flourishing town of Fulton, some thirty miles distant. Cole county, over which the eye glances looking towards the south, is neither so large, so populous, so opulent, nor so fertile as its neighbor on the opposite bank. It embraces some four hundred square miles of territory, has some seven hundred farms, and some seven thousand inhabitants.

Between the city of Jefferson and the mouth of the Missouri, a distance of nearly a hundred and forty miles, there are several towns of some importance, among which are Hermann and St. Charles. The former village is on the south bank of the Missouri, on a lofty bluff, about forty miles below the capitol, and chiefly inhabited by Germans, about nine hundred in number. The spot is noticeable for its culture of the vine. Five hundred acres of the hill-sides around it are now devoted to this department of agriculture, and the annual product of wine is said to average thirty thousand gallons.

Above Jefferson City, on the banks of the Missouri, stand several flourishing towns, among which, Booneville, about fifty miles distant, and Lexington, about twice as far, and both on the same side of the river, may be named as the chief.

The Railroad from St. Louis to the State line, now in progress, and which is already in use for more than forty miles, takes Jefferson City in its route, and cannot fail to prove of immense benefit to the place. Commenced on the 4th of July, 1851, the first division of the road was opened on the 19th of June, 1853, and it will, it is calculated, be in running order to convey members of the Legislature to the capital for the session of 1854–5. The route pursued is from St. Louis to Franklin, a distance of forty miles; thence through Gray's Gap into the Missouri Bottom and up the valley to Jefferson City, a distance of some ninety miles farther. Hence up the river bank, and under the bluffs on which stands the Capitol, it will pursue its way inland by what is called the "Johnson County Route," instead of along the river by Booneville and Lexington, as was at first contemplated.

The scene presented by our artist will be one of extreme animation, when it shall be, at once, the stopping-place for cars, and the landing-place for boats. Nothing of the city is here beheld, it is true,—its streets and houses being all of them half a mile distant, along the brow of the hill, away to the left; and yet, from no point, perhaps, could a more imposing view have been taken, than from that selected. The huge stone structure with spacious galleries, in the middle ground, is the "Missouri Hotel," beyond which, at the base of the bluff, stands a small warehouse, with the bell for the Ferry elevated on a post on the river-bank in front. Before us, in the distance, rises the lordly Capitol on its lordly bluff; while far away, from the right, comes sweeping on the still more lordly river, against the mighty current of which the strong steamers are struggling on their upward course.

ST. JOSEPH.

Not even in the broad and beautiful valley of the west is there another instance of growth so rapid as that of the town of St. Joseph, on the banks of the distant Missouri. Twenty years ago, this whole region was the unquestioned realm of the savage. Here were the villages of the Otoes, the Missouries, the Omahaws, the Santee and Yancton Sioux; and not until the autumn of 1836 was their title extinguished and regular settlement commenced. Prior to this, however, Joseph Roubadoux, Lucien Fontanelle and others, had for years resided on the frontier; and the first petition for the acquisition of that beautiful region, subsequently known as the "Platte Purchase," was drawn up by Gen. Andrew S. Hughes. That this country, centuries ago, was a favorite spot for the dwelling of men, is indicated by the remains of antiquity found on its surface, and especially by those ruins of an ancient city brought to light within a few months near the town of Parkville, in the county of Platte.

The site of St. Joseph is commanding, on the eastern bank of the Missouri, which here makes a remarkable bend, and about one mile from its shore; and, though so recent in origin that its name is to be found only on maps of latest date, it is yet boldly pronounced "The second city in the State." Whether this is, or is not now the fact, it will, in all human probability, soon become so. It is the chief town of Buchanan county, though not the capital,—a county containing some three hundred square miles of excellent soil, with a surface generally prairie, some thirteen hundred farms, and some thirteen thousand inhabitants. What the population of St. Joseph may be at this present writing, or what may be the number of its houses, is not easy to decide. It is very certain, however, that they are both far greater than they were when our artist took his view, and that they will be greater still before another summer shall have passed away. Independently of its site, as the centre of one of the most produc-

DRAWN AFTER NATURE

For the Proprietor: HERRMANN J. MEYER.

ST JOSEPH

(MISSOURI)

Published for HERRMANN J. MEYER. 164. William-Str. NEWYORK.

tive regions on the continent, and as a point at which emigration to Oregon and California will for many years make its rendezvous, there are other circumstances in its location which cannot fail to render it one of the most important places in the west. It lies on the direct route of what is regarded as the shortest and best line for a railroad from the Atlantic to the Pacific, should the South Pass be selected as the entrance to Oregon and California through the Rocky Range. From St. Joseph eastward, a chain of roads is already in contemplation, or in actual construction. The road from St. Joseph to Hannibal on the Mississippi, a distance of seventy miles through a fertile and rolling prairie abounding with coal, is already surveyed and located, and will soon be commenced. Congress has made a grant of alternate sections along its route, and the General Assembly of the State has subscribed a million and a half to its stock. The available means of the Company at the present time are estimated at two millions; and seven thousand tons of railroad iron have already been purchased. This link in the great chain to the east completed, another short one of only thirty-five miles connects it with the Northern Cross Railroad from Naples to Springfield, in Illinois. This road, it is contemplated by the Illinois Central Railroad Company to connect with their great road, by an extension of forty-five miles from Springfield to Decatur; and the addition of a few more links unites the chain with the roads of Indiana, Ohio and the east. This chain of roads completed, and the distance from St. Joseph to New York is estimated at less than twelve hundred miles. Such is the northern route. The other route, parallel to this, is from Kansas to New York *via* St. Louis, a hundred miles farther; while the advantages of the former route over the latter make the difference equivalent, it is estimated, to four times that distance. But both of these railroad chains will, in all probability, in course of time, be completed.

Be this as it may, however, the direct advantages, to be anticipated from this road, not only to St. Joseph and Hannibal, and to the immense tract of fertile and beautiful country which lies between them, but also to the commercial emporium of the State, and to the whole State itself, are incalculably great. It connects the Missouri with the Mississippi, and thus by the aid of both streams opens a direct route to market for the fertile region which stretches between, and the flourishing towns which form its termini. Under circumstances like these, therefore, if St. Joseph is not now "the second city in Missouri," it may very soon become so.

INDEPENDENCE.

About four miles south of the banks of the Missouri, and a hundred and thirty miles north-west of Jefferson City, and thrice that distance above St. Louis, stands the town of Independence, the capital of Jackson County. Thirty years ago, when the Presidential struggle between Clay and Jackson was at its height, it is related that a band of emigrants from Kentucky and other Western States, commenced a settlement on the north side of the Big Bend of the Missouri, and called their county Clay, and their capital, Liberty; while, at the same time, another band of emigrants from Virginia and other Southern States, pitched their tents on the south side of the same Big Bend, and called their county Jackson, and their capital, Independence.

For some years there existed considerable rivalry between the two county-seats; but Independence now views her young neighbor, St. Joseph, as a far more dangerous competitor than her old one, Liberty. The latter town, however, is by no means to be despised,—with its eight or nine hundred inhabitants—its three or four academies—its one or two newspapers—its court-house, jail, extensive stores and excellent landing.

The site of Independence is high, healthy, uniform and beautiful. Its communication with the interior is by means of excellent roads, and with the river by means of a railroad and other thoroughfares, penetrating the bluffs, and graded to the steamboat landing. The intervening space of some hundreds of acres has been cut up by streets into squares, and may in a few years be lined by houses. The town itself embraces an area of about one thousand acres. The value of its property as assessed, is some two millions of dollars, and its population, some four thousand. The dwellings are handsome, and chiefly of brick; the streets are regular; there is a public square, and shade trees are numerous and ornamental.

DRAWN AFTER NATURE

For the Proprietor: HERRMANN J. MEYER.

INDEPENDENCE - COURTHOUSE

(MISSOURI)

Published for HERRMANN J. MEYER. 164. William-Str. NEW YORK.

For many years Independence has been deemed the outpost of civilization, and the rendezvous or gathering-spot from which caravans and companies, whether for the purpose of exploration, emigration, or military expedition, started forth, on their long journey over the Plains to the distant West. It was a sort of port or harbor on the shore of an inland ocean, from which the squadrons of explorers, hunters, soldiers, settlers and emigrants took clearance and departure;—the distance to Santa Fe being 850 miles, and that to San Francisco, about 2,200. On this account alone, if on no other, it was destined to become a place of considerable importance. Here, outfits are now obtained, and here, as a starting point, large companies assemble. The surrounding region has many a time been perfectly whitened by the tents of travellers, unable, because of their numbers, to obtain accommodation within the houses of the town. Through this place, on its route to the mouth of the Kansas, a few miles west on the frontier line, is destined to pass the Pacific Railroad, already commenced at St. Louis; and the road when completed must greatly add to the importance of the place. If the Hudson River Railroad can compete successfully with the Hudson River, and the New York and New Haven Railroad with the East River, much more successfully can the St. Louis and Kansas Railroad compete with the turbid Missouri, "frozen up one-half of the year, and dried up the other"—always perilous and always tedious—in the navigation of which, the average speed of steamers up stream, on account of detentions and obstacles, is estimated at five miles the hour, and down stream, lying by every night, at seven.

The Kansas enters the Missouri some nine miles west of Independence, after pursuing a course due east, through the plains from the base of the Rocky Mountains, some seven or eight hundred miles. From this point to St. Louis, by the line of the railroad, the distance will be about three hundred miles, though, by the sinuosities of the rivers, nearly a hundred farther. In like manner, from Independence, due south to Galveston, in Texas, on the Mexican Gulf, it is only seven hundred miles; while, by the rivers, the distance is more than double. Most of the intervening space is prairie, and a more favorable region for a railroad, when it shall have become settled, can scarcely be found.

The business of Independence, in connection with western emigration, is already very considerable, and vast sums are here expended in procuring indispensable supplies, as well as in carrying on the small remains of the Indian trade, and that with Santa Fè. Some of its stores and places of business are extensive, and the capital invested is large. A court-house, a jail, a few places of public worship, and a couple of newspapers, constitute prominent features in its present aspect. Jackson County, of which it is the seat of justice, embraces nearly eight hundred square miles of territory, drained by the Big and Little Blue Rivers, which flow into the Missouri, with a surface elevated and undulating, well-watered and well-timbered, with a rich soil peculiarly adapted to grain and grass and which supplies the agricultural staple of Indian corn, while its rich pastures abound with stock of every description. It can boast a thousand farms, two thousand dwellings, and some fourteen thousand inhabitants. Its manufacturing establishments are about eight in number, in which are invested more than $100,000, which give employment to nearly three hundred persons, and afford an annual product of about $30,000. It was in Jackson County, that the Mormon Prophet located his Mount Zion, when he and his disciples were driven from Kirtland, Ohio, in the summer of 1836–7; and it was by the inhabitants of this county that they were driven away to Nauvoo, Illinois, in the course of the famous Mormon War which arose some years after.

A MANDAN VILLAGE.

THOSE who have examined the extensive and curious collection made by the painter, GEORGE CATLIN, some twenty or thirty years ago, during his long wanderings in the western wilds, will remember that there were in the collection, four pictures representing the strange warlike, and religious customs of the Mandan Indians. This was then, one of the most numerous and powerful of all the Indian nations between the Mississippi and the Pacific, famed alike for the prowess of its braves, in the battle and the chase. But a few years since the small-pox broke out among them. Its ravages were fearful; whole villages were destroyed; and at last there remained of the proud and mighty tribe, only a few weak and spirit-broken families. A village of these melancholy survivors was seen by our artist one afternoon on a bluff of the Upper Missouri, as his boat floated down the stream, and transferred to canvass. Ard thus it is that in these views of the United States illustrated, amid the scenes of a young empire rising to unequalled power and greatness, we present this single memento of the past, this solitary picture of an almost extinguished people, whom, with all the members of their race, the names of their habitations, will ere long have entirely disappeared from the earth.

DRAWN AFTER NATURE

For the Proprietor: HERRMANN J. MEYER

A MANDAN VILLAGE

UPPER MISSOURI

Published for HERRMANN J. MEYER. 164 William Str. NEW YORK.

DRAWN AFTER NATURE

For the Proprietor: HERRMANN J. MEYER.

THE VOLCANO - GOLDDIGGINGS

(California)

Published for HERRMANN J. MEYER. 164. William-Str. NEW-YORK.

CALIFORNIA.

An Encyclopedia, published only a few years since, which pretended to give the latest and most authentic information on the subjects of which it treated, had this to say of California: "It is a province of Mexico, on the coast of the Pacific Ocean, called by Captain Vancouver, New Albion. It lies north of the peninsula which is called Old California, and is six hundred miles long and only thirty broad. The square leagues are 2125. Monterey is the capital. There is not any country in the world which more abounds in fish and game of every description; hares, rabbits and stags are very common here; seals and otters are also found in prodigious numbers. To the northward and during the winter, the inhabitants kill a great many foxes, bears, wolves and wild-cats. The land possesses also great fertility: farinaceous roots and seeds of all kinds abundantly prosper. The crops of maize, corn and peas, cannot be equalled by those of Chili. European cultivation can have no conception of a similar fertility. The medium produce of corn is from seventy to eighty bushels per acre, the extreme, one hundred. The population, including Indians, who have begun to settle and cultivate fields, is 15,562."

This was all that was known of California a few years ago; but take up a newspaper now,—say the *Alta-California*, a folio paper, which is served daily in a city called San Francisco,—you will read in the first place a long address from a gentleman who signs himself the Governor, and who discusses the tenure of land, the establishment of a general system of education for the youth of *the State*, the federal relations of the United States, and the necessity of subscribing some twenty or thirty millions of dollars towards constructing a railroad to the Mississippi river. Secondly, you will peruse several columns of well written editorials on the politics of Europe, on the war between Turkey and Russia, on the annexation of the Sandwich Islands, on the merits of rival lines of steamers, on the moral and social qualities of Chinese citizens, on a scheme for constructing important railroads, on the excellent acting at the theatre, on the capital vocalization of the last *prima donna*, on the geological survey, on the examination in Mr. Smith's classical academy, and on the stringency of the money market. Next, you will find voluminous reports of the proceedings in courts of justice, reports from the mining districts, prices current, shipments of specie to the Atlantic coasts, and copious extracts from the journals of all parts of the world, giving news and speculation on current events. And, finally, you will run your eye along stately and imposing columns of advertisements, auctioneers, merchants, hotel-keepers, bankers, gold-diggers, jockies, artists, farmers, all offering their commodities, in liberal quantities, and at the lowest prices.

As you throw down the sheet, you exclaim, "Where am I? Can this be the California of which I read in the Encyclopedia? or is it only a dream? Has the writer of the book deceived me, or is the newspaper itself a sham? The one speaks of a scarcely inhabited country, filled with bears, foxes and wild game, and the other records the evidences of an organized and highly civilized existence! What has become of the otters, the seals and the Indians, and whence the busy multitudes of men, shops and houses that have taken their place? Surely, like Rip Van Winkle, I must have been asleep these twenty years on the mountains, and but just have awakened, with my old recollections about me, to some new and astonishing condition."

No, dear reader, you have neither been asleep nor deceived. California was, a few years ago, just what the Encyclopedia describes it to have been, and California is now just what that teeming newspaper indicates. The change is substantially real, inconceivable. Rome, contrary to the old proverb, has been built in a day. Five short revolutions of the sun have seen the foundations laid, and the complete establishment of a prosperous and populous nation,—of a nation that, drawn together by chance, has organized itself into a regular and orderly free government,—of a nation where trade, the arts and religion, flourish.

It is certainly the most marvellous thing under the heavens—this origin and progress of California. That the accidental discovery of a few grains of shining dust, which had lain for centuries unobserved upon the surface of the ground, should have moved the whole world to its centre; that it should have attracted out of all nations a host of adventurers and fortune-hunters; that these again should have come together perfect strangers, and yet formed themselves almost at once into a stable constitutional state,—are facts which now that we know and witness them, seem scarcely credible. Had they been predicted, as possible, by some modern Cassandra, she would have met Cassandra's fate, in a general disbelief. A loud laugh of derision and scorn would have gone up from every listener, and the small wits of the newspapers would have cracked endless dull jokes at the expense of the poor prophetess. Yet, California is what we see it to be,—a great and wealthy State, of many people, of several not inconsiderable cities, of courts and school-houses, and of a still more promising future.

We all remember the excitement it produced, when the first reports of the discovery of gold at Sutter's Fort were confirmed by tangible evidences of their truth. The feeling created by the earliest bulletins from Waterloo could scarcely have been more intense. Men and women of comfortable prospects at home, relinquished their old places in haste, to rush to El Dorado; merchants freighted their ships with produce to supply the wants of the thronging miners; philosophers speculated on the practical effects of an unlimited supply of money; towns were built in a week; fortunes like those which had taken centuries to accumulate, were made in a day; and all mankind fondly believed that all mankind was going to be rich. Many, indeed, were sorely disappointed, as these exaggerated expectations were not fulfilled. Still, California has grown with time, and remains the most wonderful fact of modern experience.

The first effect of the sudden supply of treasure yielded by the mines, was an almost ludicrous rise of produce. The instances narrated of the enormous value put upon the most common things, have the air of a child's fable, in which objects lose all of their ordinary proportions, and seem to lessen and expand by caprice. The rent of a house ran up to $110,000 per year; a canvas tent sold for $40,000; cellars six feet under ground let for $250 the month; an intestate's estate, before his representatives could settle his affairs, had grown to an income of $60,000 per annum; servants' wages were $200 per month; a pair of boots cost $50,—and day-laborers would often gamble away in a night, ten or twenty thousand, and return a few days after to undergo similar losses.

Yet, in the midst of this insane avidity, and wanton use of wealth, in the midst of multiplied social disorders, each man seeking for himself, and each man defending himself, the elements of order were quietly at work laying out streets, building houses, establishing laws, and concentrating families. It was not long before a political constitution, in several respects superior to any that had before existed, was devised, the State was admitted into the Union of the United States, and its representatives appeared on the floor of the National Congress. At present, too, we write books, and make pictures about California, as if it had been in being since the flood, and we were called to describe the manners, customs, and antiquities of a settled people.

The views we present on the opposite pages, were true when they were taken, but such has been the amazing rapidity of progress there, that we do not know whether our engravings may not be as much out of date as the description in the Encyclopedia which we have already quoted.

The first is of Monterey, once the capital, as we are told, but now thrown quite into the shade by the superior site of San Francisco. The view of it, as you approach from the coast side, by a road which runs through a gap between two low piny hills, is unusually fine. The houses, scattered loosely over a gentle slope, behind which runs a waving outline of pine-covered hills, are substantially built, and several of them even elegant. On the right hand, are the blue waters of the bay, quite covered with vessels, and in front, on the bluff, stand the old fort and the government houses, now surmounted by the American flag. The streets are regular and wide, and the Town Hall, in which the Constitutional Convention held its sittings, a spacious edifice of beautiful yellow stone. There is not the bustle of trade about it that one finds in San Francisco, but it is by no means a dead city like those of Italy. Its situation, both for the purposes of trade and for a residence, is admirable. The climate is delicious, and the scenery picturesque. The outline of the hills in the rear gradually merges in that of the high mountains of the coast range. Eastward, a high rocky ridge, called the Toro mountains, makes a prominent object in the view; and when the air is clear, the Sierra di Gavilau, beyond the Salinas plains, is distinctly visible.

The temperature, even in midwinter, according to Bayard Taylor, to whose El Dorado we are largely indebted for our description, is like that of May in the Eastern States, and the winds are as pleasant and balmy as those of Southern Europe. The thermometer in-doors varies from 52° to 54°, which is only 10° lower than the air without. The siroccos of other parts of the country are unknown in Monterey; the mornings are frequently foggy, but it always clears about ten o'clock, and remains clear till near sunset. The sky at noon-day is a clear, soft blue.

The harbor of Monterey is equal to any in the new State. The bight in which vessels anchor, is entirely protected from the north-westers by Seagull Point, and from the south-eastern winds by mountains in the rear. Its trade, consequently, is rapidly increasing, and when the entrance to the bay shall have been made safer by the erection of the necessary light-houses, it will become the mart of a most extensive commerce. There is also another circumstance which adds to its commercial importance. The gold placers on the Mariposa, and on the Luke Fork, King's River, and Pitiuna,—streams which empty into the Tularè lake, on the eastern side, have attracted a large mining population to the region, who must necessarily make Monterey their depot for exports and supplies.

Monterey is said to contain, with the exception of Los Angelos, the most pleasant society in California. There is a circle of families, American and Native, residing there, whose genial and refined character causes the stranger to forget his eastern home, and which corrects his first impression as to the rudeness and depravity of California life. The native population possesses great natural refinement, and has attracted about it the most desirable elements from the new-comers. It seems, however, that the crops of humanity, are quite as prolific as those of vegetable nature, and that fifteen or sixteen children is the ordinary product of a family. One gentleman rejoices in no less than thirty of these "arrows;" Mr. Hartwell, the Government translator, has twenty-one; and Senor Abrego, though married but twelve years, counted as many heirs.

DRAWN AFTER NATURE. For the Proprietor: HERRMANN J. MEYER.

MONTEREY
in California.

Published for HERRMANN J. MEYER. 164. William-Str. NEW-YORK.

Mr. Taylor in describing the natural beauties of Monterey, says:—" No one can be in Monterey a single night, without being startled and awed by the deep, solemn crashes of the surf as it breaks along the shore. There is no continuous roar of the plunging waves, as we hear on the Atlantic seaboard; the slow, regular swells—quiet pulsations of the great Pacific's heart—roll inward in unbroken lines and fall with single grand crashes, with intervals of dead silence between. They may be heard through the day, if one listens, like a solemn undertone to all the shallow noises of the town, but at midnight, when all else is still, those successive shocks fall upon the ear with a sensation of inexpressible solemnity. All the air, from the pine forests to the sea, is filled with a light tremor and the intermitting beats of sound are strong enough to jar a delicate ear. Their constant repetition at last produces a feeling something like terror. A spirit worn and weakened by some scathing sorrow could scarcely bear the reverberation.

"When there has been a gale outside, and a morning of dazzling clearness succeeds a night of fog and cold wind, the swells are loudest and most magnificent. Then their lines of foam are flung upward like a snowy fringe along the dark-blue hem of the sea, and a light, glittering mist constantly rises from the hollow curve of the shore. One quiet Sunday afternoon, when the uproar was such as to be almost felt in the solid earth, I walked out along the sand till I had passed the anchorage and could look on the open Pacific. The surface of the bay was comparatively calm; but within a few hundred yards of the shore it upheaved with a slow, majestic movement, forming a single line more than a mile in length, which, as it advanced, presented a perpendicular front of clear green water, twelve feet in height. There was a gradual curving-in of this emerald wall—a moment's waver—and the whole mass fell forward with a thundering crash, hurling the shattered spray thirty feet into the air. A second rebound followed; and the boiling, seething waters raced far up the sand with a sharp, trampling, metallic sound, like the jangling of a thousand bars of iron. I sat down on a pine log, above the highest wave-mark, and watched this sublime phenomenon for a long time. The sand-hills behind me confined and redoubled the sound, prolonging it from crash to crash, so that the ear was constantly filled with it. Once, a tremendous swell came in close on the heels of one that had just broken, and the two uniting, made one wave, which shot far beyond the water-line and buried me above the knee. As far as I could see, the shore was white with the subsiding deluge. It was a fine illustration of the magnificent language of Scripture: 'He maketh the deep to boil like a pot; he maketh the sea like a pot of ointment; one would think the deep to be hoary.'

"The pine forest behind the town encloses in its depths many spots of remarkable loneliness and beauty. The forest itself had a peculiar charm for me, and scarcely a day passed without my exploring some part of its solemn region. The old, rugged trees, blackened with many fires, are thickly bearded with long gray moss, which gives out a hoarse, dull sound as the sea-wind sweeps through them. The promontory of Monterey is entirely covered with them, excepting only the little glens, or canadas, which wind their way between the interlocking bases of the hills. Here, the grass is thick and luxuriant through the whole year; the pines shut out all sight but the mild, stainless heaven above their tops; the air is fragrant with the bay and laurel, and the light tread of a deer or whirr of a partridge, at intervals, alone breaks the delicious solitude. The far roar of the surf, stealing up through the avenues of the forest, is softened to a murmur by the time it reaches these secluded places. No more lovely hermitages for thought or the pluming of callow fancies, can be found among the pine-bowers of the Villa Borghese."

Our next view relates to the scene of the gold-washings on Monkelumne River. It is a spot to attract the artist as well as the fortune-hunter. Forming what is termed "a gulch" between the mountains, the land rises almost precipitously on every side to the distance of several hundred feet. A gentle stream meanders at the bottom, and in a bar of this are found the wet diggings. This bar is a level space at the junction of the river with a dry "arroyo" or ravine, which winds for about eight miles among the hills. It is dry and rocky, with no loose sand, except such as had lodged between the huge masses of stone, which are of course thrown aside to get at the gold. When the waters are turned off from these bars, the earth is turned up with shovels, and then thrown into a cradle, where it is separated from the gold it may contain. A flat wooden bowl is used for a second washing. Sometimes three or four pounds of the precious metal are washed out in this way, in the course of a day, but generally, the yield is not so large. Two ounces daily, is considered a handsome return for the most laborious operations. At the "dry diggings," further up the mountains, the procedure of extracting the ore is different. Gathering the loose dry sand into a bowl, they raise it to their heads and slowly pour it upon a blanket spread at their feet. Repeating this several times, and throwing out the worthless pieces of rock, they reduce the dust to about half its bulk; then, balancing the bowl on one hand, by a quick dexterous motion of the other, they cause it to revolve, at the same time throwing its contents into the air and catching them as they fall. In this manner, everything is finally winnowed away, except the heavier grains of sand mixed with the gold, which is carefully separated by the breath. It is a laborious occupation, and is chiefly confined to the natives and Indians, who are hired to do the work by the more prosperous American diggers.

The fortunes of those who undertake these washings, are as various as in other pursuits. One person will gather his "plum" in the course of a few months exertion; another will pass a year in the most active labour, and scarcely pay his expenses; in some instances, persons will dig for days, and finding nothing, will give up in despair, but scarcely have they departed, when another set of men, will strike their picks into

DRAWN AFTER NATURE

For the Proprietor: HERRMANN J. MEYER.

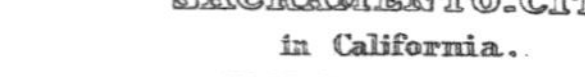

SACRAMENTO-CITY
in California.
AS IT WAS IN THE YEAR 1850.

Published by HERRMANN J. MEYER. 164. William-Str. NEW-YORK.

the same holes, and turn out the shining particles in abundance. A friend of ours encountered a happy hit of the latter kind. He arrived one morning at a gulch on the Monkelumne, and struck upon an opening, which had the day before been abandoned by a company that had expended ten or twelve days in turning up the earth with only the most indifferent success. During his first week he took out fourteen pounds of the precious stuff, and for several subsequent weeks raised in his acquisitions from six to ten pounds. He was enabled to return to the Eastern States, after a single year's labour, and now inhabits a palace on one of the New York avenues. "It is all a whirligig and a lottery," said one of his unfortunate predecessors, who still languishes somewhere in the region, as poor as when he quit a promising business in the East to seek wealth in the West,—as poor in pocket, and much poorer in spirit, health, content and manly virtue.

Our third view represents Sacramento City,—a place only second in importance to San Francisco, which must ever be, on account of its natural position, the great commercial mart of the Dorado State. It is built on the eastern bank of the river Sacramento, at its junction with the Rio Americano—languages as well as much else, are curiously mingled in the new land—embracing a square of about one-and-a-half miles in extent on each side. It is laid out in regular right-angles like the upper part of New York, the streets running east being named alphabetically, and those running west, being numbered arithmetically. But the large number of the original forest trees still standing in the midst of the town, give it quite a picturesque appearance. Indeed, many of the thoroughfares are lined on both sides with oaks and sycamores, six feet in diameter, and spreading broad leafy canopies above the heads of the passers. Beyond the waters of the Rio Americano is a noble range of hills, presenting gracefully undulating outlines, and sheltering the harbour from rude winds.

Sacramento City has the name of not being as healthful as the other cities in California, agues and diarrhœas prevailing at certain seasons of the year, but it is supposed that these will disappear with the progress of cultivation, and that it will be as salubrious as any part of the globe. Perhaps, even as it is, the rivalry of neighbouring cities, has exaggerated these unfavorable aspects. It is certain, at any rate, that it has grown with a prodigious rapidity, and that the imputed dangers have had no effect in restraining the settlement of population. It has a theatre, printing presses, saloons, hotels, shops, stores, and the other tokens of prosperity in abundance, while the prices of real estate are quite as frightful as those of

At the time Mr. Taylor visited the place, (in 1850,) it was only a few months old, and the description he gives of it is not the most flattering. Let his account of a visit to the theatre suffice for a specimen. He writes:—"At the time of which I am writing, Sacramento City boasted the only theatre in California. Its performances, three times a week, were attended by crowds of the miners, and the owners realized a very handsome profit. The canvas building used for this purpose fronted on the levee, within a door or two of the City Hotel; it would have been taken for an ordinary drinking-house, but for the sign: 'EAGLE THEATRE,' which was nailed to the top of the canvas frame. Passing through the bar-room we arrive at the entrance; the prices of admission are: Box, $3; Pit, $2. The spectators are dressed in heavy overcoats and felt hats, with boots reaching to the knees. The box-tier is a single rough gallery at one end, capable of containing about a hundred persons; the pit will probably hold three hundred more, so that the receipts of a full house amount to $900. The sides and roof of the theatre are canvas, which, when wet, effectually prevents ventilation, and renders the atmosphere hot and stifling. The drop-curtain, which is down at present, exhibits a glaring landscape, with dark-brown trees in the foreground, and lilac-colored mountains against a yellow sky.

"The overture commences; the orchestra is composed of only five members, under the direction of an Italian, and performs with tolerable correctness. The piece for the night is 'The Spectre of the Forest,' in which the celebrated actress, Mrs. Ray, 'of the Royal Theatre, New Zealand,' will appear. The bell rings; the curtain rolls up; and we look upon a forest scene, in the midst of which appears Hildebrand, the robber, in a sky-blue mantle. The foliage of the forest is of a dark-red color, which makes a great impression on the spectators and prepares them for the bloody scenes that are to follow. The other characters are a brave knight in a purple dress, with his servant in scarlet; they are about to storm the robber's hold and carry off a captive maiden. Several acts are filled with the usual amount of fighting and terrible speeches; but the interest of the play is carried to an awful height by the appearance of two spectres, clad in mutilated tent-covers, and holding spermaceti candles in their hands. At this juncture Mrs. Ray rushes in and throws herself into an attitude in the middle of the stage: why she does it, no one can tell. This movement, which she repeats several times in the course of the first three acts, has no connection with the tragedy; it is evidently introduced for the purpose of showing the audience that there is, actually, a female performer. The miners, to whom the sight of a woman is not a frequent occurrence, are delighted with these passages and applaud vehemently.

"In the closing scenes, where Hildebrand entreats the heroine to become his bride, Mrs. Ray shone in all her glory. 'No!' said she, 'I'd rather take a basilisk and wrap its cold fangs around me, than be clasped in the hembraces of an 'artless robber.' Then, changing her tone to that of entreaty, she calls upon the knight in purple, whom she declares to be 'me 'ope—me only 'ope!' We will not stay to hear the songs and duetts which follow; the tragedy has been a sufficient infliction. For her ''art-rending' personations, Mrs. Ray received $200 a week, and the wages of the other actors were in the same proportion. A musical gentleman was paid $96 for singing 'The Sea! the Sea!' in a deep bass voice. The usual sum paid musicians was $16 a night.

DRAWN AFTER NATURE.

Ad. Rottmann sc.

For the Proprietor: HERRMANN J. MEYER.

GOLDDIGGINS ON THE MOKELUMNE RIVER

in California.

Published for HERRMANN J. MEYER. 164 William-Str. NEW-YORK.

A Swiss organ-girl, by playing in the various hells, accumulated $4000 in the course of five or six months."

But under the advancing prosperity of the place, art has improved, and the citizens now are the patrons of Biscaccianti, Catharine Hays, Mrs. Sinclair, Mr. Murdock, and other equally celebrated histrionic and operatic performers.

Our last engraving exhibits the site of an extinct volcano on the top of the Bulte, which appears to have had several openings for the flames. The rocks have been thrown, by upheaval, into irregular cones, and show every where marks of intense heat. Large seams, blackened by the subterranean fire, run through them; and on the highest parts are round, smooth holes, a foot in diameter, to which no bottom can be found. These are evidently the last flues through which the air and flame made their way, as the surface hardened over the cooling mass. The Indian traditions go back to a time when the craters were active, but their chronology is totally indefinite. Pines at least a century old are now growing in their ruins, and further up the mountains are large beds of lava, surrounding craters of still larger dimensions. As gold in large quantities is found throughout the region, we may imagine that the early Indians who inhabited the deep bowels of the earth have forged the valuable metal, and then sent it coursing down to the valleys below. At any rate, as the geologists refuse to give us any more satisfactory account of the origin of it, and of the causes of its abundance, we have a right to assume that ours is as good a theory as any—until a better one is invented.

WESTON.

THIS rapidly growing town is on the left bank of the Missouri River, at a short bend, in the County of Platte. When the State of Missouri was first organized, the western boundary extended due north and south from the embouchure of the Kansas River. At a subsequent period, it was found, that by an extension of the line of the northern boundary of the State, due west to the Missouri River, it would strike that stream in such a direction, as to leave a long triangular strip of territory, unsuitable for attachment to any future State. By the consentaneous action of the Legislature of Missouri and the Congress of the United States, about twenty years since, this tract was annexed to Missouri. From a small river running southward, and near its eastern border, it has been called Platte County. This tract is well watered by numerous springs and small streams, the soil is exceedingly fertile, and the land proportionally divided into forest and prairie. It is well settled, and the richest farming district in the State. WESTON, is one of its principal landings on the Missouri, about forty miles above the mouth of the Kansas, and five miles above Fort Leavenworth, a military station on the right bank in the Indian Territory. This is another place of outfit and departure for the California, Oregon, and other Western emigrants. It now contains about three thousand inhabitants, and is increasing annually in population, business and trade with the rich agricultural country in the rear. There is a bend in the river, as shown in the engraving, in front of the town. The landing is an excellent one, and the harbor deep and commodious.

The Presbyterian Church to be seen in the engraving is on elevated ground in a central position. Baptists, Methodists and Roman Catholics, have houses of worship erected since our sketch was taken. The country on the opposite side of the river belongs to the Shawanese and Delaware Indians, among whom a band of Stockbridge Indians and Mun sees reside. These Indians are in a good degree civilized, cultivate farms, live in good houses, and have schools and churches, and should Nebraska territory be organized, they will probably enjoy the privilege of citizenship.

DRAWN AFTER NATURE. For the Proprietor: HERRMANN J. MEYER.

WESTON

(MISSOURI)

Published for HERRMANN J. MEYER. 164 William-Str. NEWYORK.

Vol. 1. PARTS 8 & 9. 10 Price $1.50.

THE

UNITED STATES

ILLUSTRATED;

IN

VIEWS

OF

CITY AND COUNTRY.

WITH

DESCRIPTIVE AND HISTORICAL ARTICLES,

EDITED

BY

CHARLES A. DANA.

THE WEST.

NEW YORK:—HERRMANN J. MEYER.

The present number completes the First Volume of the great National Pictorial,

THE UNITED STATES ILLUSTRATED,

comprising two Sections, the East or Seaboard States, and West, or Valley of the Mississippi and Pacific, in two separate Volumes, each containing 40 Steel Engravings, an engraved allegoric title page, and about 200 pages of letter press.

The Two Volumes forming a Superb Holiday Gift,

are to be had at the following prices:

Bound in English muslin, embossed sides and gilt edges,		**$12 00**
do	**Turkey morocco,**	**14 00**
do	**French Calf,** (in cases,)	**16 00**

Each purchaser of the two Volumes is entitled to receive the splendid picture,

THE BATTLE OF BUNKER HILL,

AFTER TRUMBULL

as a Premium.

The second Volume of the United States Illustrated is in preparation, and the first number will be laid before the Public in due time.

☞ Orders by Mail will be promptly attended to, and the Plates warranted to come safe to hand.

Address,

HERRMANN J. MEYER, Publisher.

New York, 164 William Street.

☞ With this Number the Premium Plate will be delivered to each Subscriber.

www.ingramcontent.com/pod-product-compliance
Lightning Source LLC
LaVergne TN
LVHW011203110826
845150LV00006B/1303